Plätze Urban squares

Plätze und städtische Freiräume von 1993 bis heute
Recent European promenades, squares and city centres

Edition Topos

Callwey Verlag
München

Birkhäuser
Basel · Boston · Berlin

Inhalt
Table of contents

Jarmers Plads, Copenhagen
Architects Brandt Hell Hansted Holscher
Photo: Jens Lindhe

Topos

Robert Schäfer

Die europäische Stadt definiert sich über ihre Freiräume. Eine banale Aussage, die jedoch Planer und Architekten zwingt, sich intensiv mit der Stadt und ihren Funktionen auseinanderzusetzen. "Topos – European Landscape Magazine" berichtet seit 1992 über aktuelle Ansätze der Stadtentwicklung, stellt Projekte vor und zur Diskussion. Im Mittelpunkt steht stets die Frage, wie durch den Freiraum die Stadt zu gestalten ist. Große Bedeutung kommt dabei dem Platz zu, der im Idealfall perfekt funktioniert, weil er allen Ansprüchen gerecht wird. Es gibt klassische Beispiele wie den Campo von Siena oder die Piazza Navona in Rom, die in Planerkreisen stets zitiert werden.

In diesem Buch präsentieren wir eine Reihe Plätze der jüngsten Planungsgeschichte, bekannte und weniger bekannte. In der Zusammenstellung wird die Vielfalt deutlich, die den Reiz der europäischen Städte ausmacht. Kein Platz ist wie der andere, nur wenig ist übertragbar. Wo sich der vielberufene Geist des Ortes nicht ausmachen lässt, liegt es am Architekten, durch einen überzeugenden Entwurf Identität zu schaffen. Auch wenn digitale Netze völlig neue Realitäten und Welten schaffen – ein gelungener Platz ist immer noch die beste Visitenkarte. Auf ihr steht, welche Ansprüche ernst genommen werden. Der Modellfall Barcelona wurde ausgiebig erforscht. Auch in Lyon lässt sich studieren, was machbar ist, wenn politischer Wille auf eine kompetente Verwaltung und kreative Planer trifft, zumal zu Zeiten, wenn gerade mal Geld im Stadtsäckel ruht. Der Schouwburgplein in Rotterdam gilt als Ikone moderner Platzgestaltung. Schon der Entwurf wurde heftig diskutiert, was durchaus als gutes Zeichen gewertet werden kann in einer demokratischen Gesellschaft.

Was haben wohl alle Plätze gemein? Sie sind Teil einer umfassenden Verkehrsplanung, sei es im Falle der Sanierung und Neugestaltung oder bei der selteneren Neuanlage. Weder Parkplatz noch Straßenkreuzung erfüllen die ihnen zugedachten vielfältigen Aufgaben. So stand in Lyon ein Verkehrsplan am Anfang, der die Plätze über neuen Tiefgaragen erst ermöglichte. Der einst verkehrsreiche Potsdamer Platz im Herzen Berlins steht symbolisch für ein Bündel von Fragen an Plätze, ja an den öffentlichen Raum allgemein. Können Shopping Malls als scheinöffentliche Räume den klassischen Platz ersetzen? Was erwarten die Bürger von einem zentralen Platz, wenn ihnen der Sinn gerade nicht nach Geldausgeben steht? Braucht die Stadt des 21. Jahrhunderts noch Plätze als Treffpunkt, Kundgebungsort und Festwiese? Vielleicht wird es den Platz als Klassiker der Stadtplanung bald gar nicht mehr geben? Vielleicht lassen sich die immer stärker auseinanderdriftenden Ansprüche der Nutzergruppen nicht mehr unter einen Hut bringen? Vielleicht eignen sich spontan entstehende, sich dynamisch verändernde Lücken im Stadtgewebe besser? Fragen, denen sich Planer stellen müssen. Sicher ist es spannend, einige der hier vorgestellten Plätze gelegentlich aufzusuchen. Als Besucher, Flaneur, Skater oder Gast eines Straßencafés wird man merken, ob alles passt, am Platz, an Ort und Stelle.

European cities are defined by their open spaces. This may be a commonplace but it forces planners and architects to examine the city and its functions very closely. Topos: European Landscape Magazine has been reporting on current approaches to urban development since 1992, introducing projects and putting them up for discussion. The main focus is always on the question of how to shape the city by means of open space. Public squares are extremely important in this respect. In ideal cases they function perfectly because they satisfy all requirements. Classic examples, such as the Campo in Siena or Piazza Navona in Rome, are constantly being cited by professional planners.

This book presents a series of squares, both familiar and less well known, dating from the recent history of planning. Assembling them in this way emphasises their variety, which is what constitutes the charm of European cities. No square is like any other; hardly any feature is transferable. Wherever the much cited genius loci is not obvious, it is the architect's responsibility to create identity with a convincing design. While digital networks may create completely new realities and worlds, a successful square is still a city's best calling card. It indicates what demands are taken seriously. The model of Barcelona has been researched thoroughly. Lyon too provides an opportunity to study what can be done when the political will encounters a competent administration and creative planners, particularly at a time when the municipal purse happens not to be empty. Rotterdam's Schouwburgplein is considered the icon of modern form for a square. Even its design was fiercely debated, which counts as a good sign in a democratic society.

What might all these squares have in common? They are all part of a comprehensive traffic plan, whether connected to urban renewal and redesign or, more rarely, to new development. Neither parking lots nor intersections serve the various purposes assigned to squares. In Lyon the traffic plan made squares atop the new underground car parks possible in the first place. Potsdamer Platz in the heart of Berlin, formerly crowded with traffic, stands for a whole cluster of questions to ask about squares, and even about public space in general. Can shopping malls as pseudo public spaces replace the classic square? What do people want in a centrally located place when they don't happen to be in the mood for spending money? Does the city of the 21st century still need squares as meeting places, festival grounds and venues for public announcements?

Perhaps the square as the classical element in urban planning will soon cease to exist. Perhaps the increasingly diverse requirements of its user groups can no longer be accommodated in one place. Perhaps spontaneously arising, dynamically changing gaps in the urban fabric are more suitable. These are questions that planners should be asking themselves. It will certainly continue to be exciting to seek out some of the squares in this book from time to time. Visiting, perambulating, skating, or patronising a sidewalk café on site, you will soon find out if they still work as squares.

Lyon und Saint-Etienne: Politik für den öffentlichen Raum

Lyon and Saint-Etienne: public space policies

Jean-Pierre Charbonneau

Lyon gilt als Pionierstadt für die Neugestaltung städtischer Freiräume. Nun entwickelt auch Saint-Etienne seinen eigenen Stil.

Lyon is considered a pioneer in the new design of urban open spaces. Saint-Etienne is developing its own style with young planners.

Wieso sollte Stadtplanung eine abstrakte Wissenschaft bleiben, die nur schematisch die Entwicklung einer Stadt und ihrer Viertel vorsieht, während eine andere Disziplin – die Architektur – die Schemata mit Gebäuden ausfüllt, und der Rest, also der Freiraum, den Fachingenieuren überlassen wird, um dort Leitungen und Autotrassen hineinzupressen? Wohl beschwören viele den Tod des öffentlichen Raums. Dennoch, meine ich, spielt sich ein Großteil unseres gesellschaftlichen Lebens dort ab. Man braucht nur durch die ungestalten Freiräume von Großwohnsiedlungen zu gehen, um die gähnende Leere zu erleben zwischen Gebäuden, die aussehen wie Würfelzucker auf einer Tischplatte. Sitzt man jedoch auf einem beliebigen, noch so kleinen Stadtplatz mitten in Paris, dann kommt einem wieder in den Sinn, wie stark die Gestaltung des öffentlichen Raumes das Leben in der Stadt beeinflußt.

Das Beispiel Lyon. In Lyon nahm sich Henry Chabert, Baudezernent und Vizepräsident des Nachbarschaftsverbandes »Grand Lyon«, diese Erkenntnis zu Herzen und setzte 1989 eine Politik zur Ordnung des öffentlichen Raumes in Gang – mich beauftragte er mit der Umsetzung. Unser Plan war, pro Jahr zehn Freiräume zu gestalten, und zwar verteilt im ganzen Stadtgebiet: in der Altstadt und in den sozial schwachen Vierteln, auf bestehenden Plätzen und Boulevards, in den Neubauvierteln wie der Cité Internationale *(siehe Topos 10)* und an neuen Verkehrsknotenpunkten. Bis heute realisierten wir 200 Projekte – doppelt so viele wie ursprünglich geplant. Wir ergriffen jede Gelegenheit, so zum Beispiel die Neuordnung der Grundstücke entlang der neuen Métro-Linie. Selbstverständlich erforderte dieses Mammutvorhaben eine detaillierte Überwachung sämtlicher Projekte vom Entwurf über die Planung bis hin zur Ausführung. Dafür schufen wir in den Ämtern der Stadt und des Nachbarschaftsverbandes (mit Jean-Louis Azéma als Direktor) mehrere Planungskomitees. Jeweils einem Projektleiter wurde die Verantwortung für einen Ort übertragen, er vermittelte zwischen Planern, Firmen und den zahlreichen Ämtern. Er stellte das Raumprogramm auf, führte Entscheidungen herbei und organisierte die Bauleitung. Entwurf und Bauleitung lagen fast immer in der Hand von freien Planern, nicht in der von Generalunternehmern oder öffentlichen Stellen. So konnten wir die Rollen klar verteilen – auf der einen Seite

Why should urban planning remain an abstract science, only developing a city and its districts schematically, while another discipline, namely architecture, fills in the schemata with buildings and leaves the rest, that is, the open space, over to the engineers to squeeze in conduits and roads? Many people believe in the death of public space. In my opinion, most of our social life still takes place in it. You only need to walk through the planless open spaces in large-scale urban developments to experience the absolute emptiness between buildings that look like sugar cubes on a bare table. On the other hand, if you sit in one of the squares in the middle of Paris, no matter how small, you will be reminded of how much the design of public space affects life in the city.

The Lyon example. In Lyon the head of the urban planning department and vice-president of the community association "Grand Lyon," Henry Chabert, took this realisation to heart. He set out to establish a public space policy in 1989 and commissioned me to execute it. Our plan was to design ten open spaces a year throughout the urban area: in the historic city centre and the socially challenged districts, on existing squares and boulevards, in the new developments such as Cité Internationale (see *Topos* 10) and at new traffic junctions. So far we have completed 200 projects, twice as many as originally planned. We took advantage of every opportunity, such as the reorganisation of lots along the new underground line. Of course this mammoth task called for detailed supervision of all projects from the design stage through the planning to the execution. To this end, we created several planning committees in the municipal departments and the communi-

Pro Jahr zehn Freiräume gestalten. So lautete das ehrgeizige Programm, das der Baudezernent von Lyon, Henry Chabert, 1989 in Gang setzte, um den öffentlichen Raum zu ordnen. Über 200 Projekte wurden es schließlich, doppelt so viele wie geplant.

Der Börsenplatz, Place da la Bourse, wurde 1993 auf einer Tiefgarage angelegt und sollte eine deutliche gärtnerische Note bekommen. Landschaftsarchitekt Alexandre Chemetoff setzte riesige mit Buchs bepflanzte Tontöpfe in Reihen, ergänzt mit Rhododendren.

Designing ten open spaces a year. That was the ambitious programme established by the head of the Lyon urban planning department, Henry Chabert, in 1989 to order the public space. Over 200 projects came about, twice as many as planned.
Place de la Bourse, the square

in front of the stock exchange, had been built above the underground carpark in 1993. It was now to be given a garden touch. The landscape architect Alexandre Chemetoff added rows of gigantic clay planters with boxwood, completing his design with rhododendrons.

Durch die Flüsse und die umgebende Hügelkette ist die Natur in Lyon stets präsent. Um jedoch mehr Grün in die Stadt zu bringen, erhielt der Pariser Landschaftsarchitekt Gilles Clément 1996 den Auftrag für einen »plan de végétalisation«, einen Begrünungsplan für Straßen und Plätze sowie Pocket parks.
Den Pflanzen sollte eine neue Rolle im Kontext der Stadt zugewiesen werden. Nicht nur Platanen können den Straßenrand zieren, auch Gräser und Sträucher bekommen ihren Platz.

The rivers and surrounding chain of hills make nature omnipresent in Lyon. Nevertheless, to bring more green into the city the Paris landscape architect Gilles Clément was commissioned in 1996 to design a "végétalisation" plan for greenery in the streets and squares and for pocket parks. Plane trees are not the only vegetation that can decorate a street. Even grasses and shrubs have a place.

ty association (with Jean-Louis Azéma as the director). One project head was responsible for one site each in order to mediate between planners, construction companies and numerous municipal offices. He set up the open space programme, brought about decision-making, and organised the supervision of building works. Design and supervision of building works were almost always in the hands of free-lance planners, not of the general contractors or the public sector. We were thus able to assign roles clearly, with professional realisation on the one hand and responsible building sponsors on the other.

With such a large number of projects, decision-making had to be precisely organised. Efficiency is essential especially because the many parties entitled to a say in how public space is designed generate many conflicting opinions. We therefore formed a pilot group, headed by Henry Chabert, which brought together everyone concerned by a given project. All programmes were assessed at their weekly, later monthly, meetings. These meetings quickly became the core of a new kind of planning for the technical professionals, municipal authorities, supervisors of the building works and even for the residents.

In order to make the various projects consistent, we established a public space vocabulary from the start. Design unity was to come about through the use of the same materials and the same street furniture, designed by the Parisian designer Wilmotte, throughout the entire conurbation. This also simplifies the maintenance of the new public spaces, although with so many new ones the public maintenance firms need to reorganise their services completely. At this point I would like to sidetrack to a few thoughts on the effects of open space policy with which almost everyone in Lyon would agree. The first step should be to get to know a site. How could the same projects be built with the same materials all over France and so many cities thus deny their history and their unique features? How many towns in the Rhône valley turn their backs on the river? Didn't it form their culture, their social structure, their economics? How could the virtues of simplicity have been forgotten all over France, the plain streets with their residential buildings, the avenues of linden trees, the overgrown roadsides and the stone walls? Instead, the blind arcades that lead nowhere should be removed, as well as the pergolas which will never be covered with climbers. In Lyon we preferred designs that subtly emphasized the characteristics of the site. We learned about the latter from observations which we recorded in plans, such as for the riverbank, for mobility, and for the peninsula between the Rhône and the Saône. The vocabulary for vegetation and street furniture was determined on the basis of historical, sociological and literary analyses of each of the sites to be redesigned.

Our design enthusiasm should not let us lose sight of how the themes and places of a city are interdependent. Hence the policy for a socially challenged district is closely related to the policy of a city as a whole. It seems pointless to advance retail trade next door to a supermarket. The municipalities of greater Lyon have therefore established a masterplan for trade development which does not permit the construction of new shopping malls. At the same time, in the framework of so-called Social Urban Development programme, 18 existing shopping centres in challenged neighbourhoods are being restructured in

eine professionelle Bauausführung, auf der anderen eine verantwortungsbewußte Bauherrschaft. Bei den zahlreichen Projekten wurde die genaue Organisation von Entscheidungen notwendig, gerade weil beim Gestalten des öffentlichen Raumes viele das Mitspracherecht haben und deshalb viele Meinungen aufeinanderprallen. Also bildeten wir eine Führungsgruppe unter der Leitung von Henry Chabert, die sämtliche an einem Projekt beteiligen Personen zusammenbrachte. Auf diesen zunächst wöchentlichen, später monatlichen Versammlungen wurden sämtliche Programme begutachtet. Die Versammlung wurde schnell zum Kern einer neuen Planungskultur für Techniker, Stadträte, Bauleiter und selbst für die Bewohner.

Wir legten von Anfang an ein Vokabular für den öffentlichen Raum fest, um eine Linie in die unterschiedlichen Projekte zu bringen. Eine gestalterische Einheit sollte entstehen durch gleiche Materialien und Baustoffe in der gesamten Stadt, und durch das Stadtmobiliar, das der Pariser De-

Saint-Etienne am Massif Central hat sich in den vergangenen 25 Jahren gewandelt. Während die Großindustrie der 200 000-Einwohner-Stadt den Rücken kehrte, siedelten sich mittelständische Unternehmen an. Um das Zentrum aufzuwerten, gab der Bürgermeister einen Entwicklungsplan in Auftrag. Vorrangig sollten funktionierende Mischquartiere entstehen und der Verkehr neu geordnet werden. Das Rückgrat der Stadt, die Grand-Rue, quert den Rathausplatz und den Platz Jean-Jaurés. Die Neugestaltung des Rathausplatzes bietet den Fußgängern mehr Bewegungsraum. Die Landschaftsarchitekten der Gruppe In Situ aus Lyon betonten die Linearität der Straßenbahngleise und ordneten den Straßenraum der Grand-Rue neu.

signer Wilmotte entwarf. Dadurch wird auch der Unterhalt der neuen Freiräume einfacher, selbst wenn sich die Pflegeabteilungen bei so vielen neuen Orten neu organisieren müssen.

Auswirkungen der Freiraumpolitik. Zunächst gilt es, sich eines Ortes bewußt zu werden. Wie soll man erklären, daß überall in Frankreich sich ähnelnde Projekte mit gleichen Materialien gebaut werden, und daß viele Städte so ihre Geschichte und ihre Besonderheiten verleugnen? Wieviele Orte im Rhônetal kehren dem Fluß ihren Rücken zu? Hat er denn nicht ihre Kultur geformt, ihr Gesellschaftsgefüge, ihre Wirtschaft? Wie konnte in ganz Frankreich die Tugend des Einfachen ignoriert werden, die einfachen Straßen mit ihren Wohnhäusern, die Lindenalleen, die bewachsenen Straßenränder und die Steinmauern? Vielmehr gehören die vorgeblendeten Arkaden abgeschafft, die nirgends hinführen, ebenso die Pergolen, über die niemals Pflanzen ranken. In Lyon bevorzugten wir die Entwürfe, die diskret die Eigenschaften eines Ortes betonen. Unser Wissen haben wir durch Beobachtungen erlangt, die wir in Plänen festhielten (Uferplan, Mobilitätsplan, Plan für die Halbinsel zwischen Rhône und Saône). Das Vokabular für Pflanzen und Stadtmobiliar bestimmten wir nach historischen, soziologischen und literarischen Analysen eines jeden Ortes, den wir für eine Umgestaltung ausgesucht hatten.

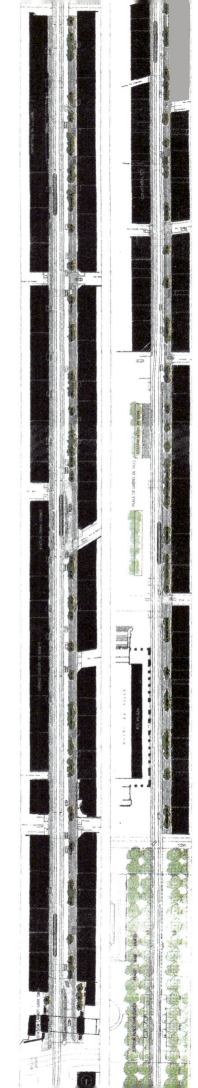

co-operation with the state, urban communities, chambers of commerce and private initiatives. This project is supported by the EU under the auspices of the URBAN programme.

Mutual dependence can also have positive effects. Catherine Foret's sociological study demonstrated that Rue de la République in Lyon's downtown pedestrian zone was where suburban youth meets to socialize. This is where they get to know the city and urban life. The renewal of this axis therefore took care to retain its status quo for the young people. This was directly opposed to another proposal to open it to traffic and recreate the original representative avenue of the beginning of this century. This example shows the need for research on the city as a whole and for treating the centre and the suburbs as one unit. Those in charge of the projects in the centre are just as highly qualified as those working on the subsidized housing developments in the suburbs. While they have the same financial resources, those in the challenged districts, however, call for more human resources because of the more complex problems to be solved. Social Urban Development is now working on 23 large housing developments in the Lyon agglomeration.

We also set up several guidelines. One was not to create inflexible open spaces but to leave them capable of development so that they can be enlivened by the residents. To begin with, many of our project areas needed to be cleaned up, traffic redirected and parking spots reorganised to make room in the first place. We also limited technical facilities such as telephone booths or newsstands to stop their usual proliferation. Nevertheless, the demand for places that are not too predetermined needs to be adapted to the complexity of a con-

Saint-Etienne in the Massif Central, which has a population of 200,000, has undergone quite a change over the last 25 years. While major industry turned its back on the city, medium-sized firms moved in. In order to upgrade the city centre, the mayor commissioned a development plan. Its main priorities are to create well functioning sites with mixed uses and a new traffic structure. The backbone of the city, an avenue named Grand-Rue, crosses the city hall and Jean-Jaurés squares. The city hall square's new design makes more room for pedestrians. The landscape architects of the In Situ group of Lyon emphasize the linearity of the tramway tracks and reorganise the street space of Grand-Rue.

Bei aller Gestaltungslust darf nicht vergessen werden, wie sich Themen und Orte einer Stadt gegenseitig beeinflussen. So ist die Politik für sozial schwache Viertel eng mit der gesamten Politik einer Stadt verbunden. Es erscheint unnötig, den Einzelhandel eines Viertels zu fördern, wenn gleich daneben ein Supermarkt gebaut wird. Deshalb haben die Gemeinden des Großraums Lyon einen Leitplan zur Entwicklung des Handels verabschiedet, der den Bau von neuen Einkaufszentren untersagt. Gleichzeitig werden im Rahmen der sogenannten sozialen Stadtentwicklung 18 bestehende Einkaufszentren in schwachen Stadtteilen umstrukturiert, in Zusammenarbeit von Staat, Kommunen, Handelskammer und privaten Initiativen. Dieses Projekt erhält Mittel von der EU im Rahmen des URBAN-Programms.

Gegenseitige Abhängigkeit kann sich auch positiv auswirken. Catherine Forets soziologische Studie stellte die zentrale Fußgängerzone Lyons, die Rue de la République, als entscheidenden Sozialisationspunkt für Jugendliche aus den Vororten heraus. Hier lernen sie die Stadt und ihr Leben kennen. Bei der Sanierung der Achse wurde deshalb genau darauf geachtet, daß sie den Jugendlichen erhalten blieb – im Gegensatz zum Wunsch, sie dem Verkehr zu öffnen und die ursprüngliche Prachtstraße vom Anfang des Jahrhunderts wiederherzustellen. Dieses Beispiel zeigt die Notwendigkeit, die gesamte Stadt zu betrachten und das Zentrum und die Vororte einheitlich zu behandeln. Die Verantwortlichen für die Projekte im Zentrum haben die gleiche Qualifikation wie diejenigen, die an den großen Wohnanlagen arbeiten. Bei dem selben Finanzaufwand wie im Zentrum ist allerdings in den sozial schwachen Gebieten mehr Einsatz nötig, um die komplexen Probleme zu lösen. Heute sind 23 Großwohnsiedlungen im Ballungsgebiet von Lyon in das Programm der sozialen Stadtentwicklung eingebunden.

Wir stellten mehrere Leitgedanken zum öffentlichen Raum auf. Einer besagt, keine starren Freiräume zu schaffen, sondern sie entwicklungsfähig zu lassen, so daß sie von den Bewohnern belebt werden können. Zunächst mußten viele unserer Projektgebiete aufgeräumt, die Verkehrsführung neu geregelt, die Parkplätze neu angeordnet werden, um überhaupt Platz zu schaffen. Wir führten auch eine Kontrolle für den Bau von Technikgebäuden wie Telefonkabinen oder Trafohäuschen ein, um den üblichen Wildwuchs zu verhindern. Der Anspruch, die Orte nicht allzusehr vorzubestimmen, muß auch der Komplexität einer zeitgenössischen Stadt angepaßt werden, unter Berücksichtigung aller Fortbewegungsmittel, der technischen Verflechtung, der unterschiedlichen Akteure und der vielschichtigen

temporary city. The means of transportation, technical infrastructures, the variety of people involved and the diversity of the population must all be taken into consideration. A city is like a live body. If you don't realise that, it will soon turn into a museum.

Another guideline was that a public place cannot suddenly be made into a venue for community life by decree. Nevertheless, it should be set up so as not to exclude certain activities and persons from the start. Safeguarding social variety calls for great sensitivity in planning as well as execution. It is always a source of conflict, as in the following case: setting up benches was actually turned down because they would give tramps a place to settle. As if the city were not also a place where the homeless have their place, even in public spaces. On the other hand, of course conflict is preprogrammed if benches in residential districts are placed under the windows, where noisemakers could be hanging out until two in the morning.

A further guideline was our attempt to create open spaces that are contemporary, not replicas of the 19th century imitating the ancient agora. We therefore collaborated with planners, artists, landscape architects and designers who contributed their contemporary touches and inventiveness. Last but not least the residents played a key role that is all too often unappreciated. Seeing as how we are increasingly working on pre-existing urban structures, every decision needs to be discussed in public and beyond ideological standpoints. Thanks to our experience in Lyon, we developed a professionalism based on certain rules. For example, no more discussions are held once a design has been approved, meetings must include representatives from all sectors of the population, etc. Behind all this is the conviction that no one person alone can dispose over the city and the lives of other people any more. The technicians, supervisors of the building works, intellectuals and politicians should all consider themselves participants in a complex process in which they devise solutions, exchange views and sometimes even argue.

The Saint-Etienne example. In Saint-Etienne, an industrial city in the southern French Massif Central mountain range, the city fathers initiated a policy for upgrading the districts. The top priority is to instill new life in the city centre because for the last few years its residents have gravitated to the adjacent rural communities where the quality of life seems better. Saint-Etienne has undergone enormous economic change in the past 25 years. Medium-sized businesses established themselves while most of the large companies closed down. Comparable cities in Europe have become considerably less important. Saint-Etienne, however, knew how to mobilize its money and energy but did so at the expense of environmental quality. Speedy and effective improvement is now planned. Mayor Michel Thiollière commissioned a development plan for the city centre to create attractive and functional mixed-use sites. Studies for several central squares followed, as well as for tramway renewal, a new traffic system, the construction of the Bellevue traffic junction and the area around the stadium. Of course the city also had to invest effort and funding in the peripheral areas. With the express support of the mayor, I proposed a strategy to develop district by district. In the face of the trend to move out of the city, action had to be quick and cover the entire urban area. Costs had to be low.

Bevölkerung. Eine Stadt ist wie ein lebendiger Körper – wenn man das nicht einsieht, verstaubt sie schnell zum Museum.

Ein anderer Leitgedanke: Natürlich kann ein öffentlicher Platz nicht per Dekret zum Ort gemeinschaftlichen Lebens ausgerufen werden. Dennoch sollten Plätze bestimmte Aktivitäten und Personen nicht von vornherein ausschließen. Die Wahrung sozialer Vielfalt erfordert viel Feingefühl bei der Planung, aber auch bei der Ausführung. Dabei gibt es immer wieder Konflikte, wie die folgende Anekdote verdeutlicht: Da wurden doch Bänke unter dem Vorwand abgelehnt, daß sie Pennern Platz böten. Als ob die Stadt nicht auch ein Ort wäre, wo Obdachlose ihren Platz finden können, und sei es im öffentlichen Raum. Allerdings ist Streit vorprogrammiert, wenn man in Wohngebieten unter die Fenster der Häuser Bänke stellt, auf denen Jugendliche dann bis zwei Uhr früh lärmen.

Ein weiterer Leitgedanke ist schließlich unser Bestreben, zeitgenössische Freiräume zu schaffen – keine Blendwerke des 19. Jahrhunderts, die die antike Agora nachäffen. Wir arbeiteten deshalb in Lyon mit Planern, Künstlern, Landschaftsarchitekten und Designern zusammen, die ihre zeitgenössische Handschrift und Erfindungsgabe einbrachten. Und nicht zuletzt spielen die Bürger eine Schlüsselrolle, die oft verkannt wird. Heute, da wir immer stärker im bestehenden Stadtgefüge arbeiten, muß jede Entscheidung in der Öffentlichkeit diskutiert werden, jenseits ideologischer Standpunkte. Durch unsere Erfahrungen in Lyon eigneten wir uns nach und nach eine Professionalität an, die auf Regeln beruht wie etwa derjenigen, daß keine Besprechungen mehr nach Verabschiedung eines Entwurfs geführt werden, oder daß bei Versammlungen Vertreter sämtlicher Bevölkerungsschichten anwesend sind. Hinter all diesen Erkenntnissen steht schließlich die Überzeugung, daß niemand mehr ganz allein die Fachkenntnis für komplexe Stadtprojekte besitzt, daß niemand mehr allein über die Stadt und über das Leben anderer verfügen kann. Die Techniker, Bauleiter, Intellektuellen, Politiker – alle sollten sich in einen vielschichtigen Prozeß eingebunden sehen, in dem sie Lösungen erfinden, austauschen und sich manchmal auch streiten.

Das Beispiel Saint-Etienne. In Saint-Etienne, einer Industriestadt im südfranzösischen Gebirge Massif Central, haben die Stadtväter eine Politik zur Aufwertung der Quartiere initiiert. Vorrangig soll das Stadtzentrum neu belebt werden, denn seit einigen Jahren zieht es die Stadtbewohner in die umliegenden Gemeinden aufs Land, weil dort angeblich die Lebensqualität

besser sei. Zur Erläuterung: Seit 25 Jahren hat Saint-Etienne einen erstaunlichen wirtschaftlichen Wandel durchgemacht. Mittelständische Unternehmen etablierten sich, während die meisten Großunternehmen schlossen. In Europa haben vergleichbare Städte enorm an Wichtigkeit verloren. Saint-Etienne verstand es jedoch, Geld und Energie zu bewahren. Dies geschah auf Kosten der Umweltqualität – jetzt soll schnell und wirkungsvoll diese Seite der Stadt verbessert werden. Der Bürgermeister Michel Thiollière gab einen Entwicklungsplan für das Zentrum in Auftrag, um dort attraktive und funktionstüchtige Mischquartiere zu schaffen. Es folgten Studien über mehrere zentrale Plätze, die Renovierung der Straßenbahnlinie, eine neue Verkehrsführung, den Bau des neuen Verkehrsknotens von Bellevue und das Umfeld des Stadions. Selbstverständlich mußte die Stadt zudem Energie und Geld in ihre Randgebiete stecken. Mit ausdrücklicher Unterstützung des Bürgermeisters schlug ich eine Strategie vor: die Quartiersentwicklung. In Anbetracht der Stadtflucht sollte schnell und im ganzen Stadtgebiet gehandelt werden, die Kosten mußten niedrig bleiben. Bei der Planung und Umsetzung halfen mir zwei wichtige Punkte: einerseits die starke Verbundenheit der Einwohner und der Verwaltung mit ihrer Stadt, einer populären und äußerst diskreten Stadt, in der man nichts zur Schau stellen mag; andererseits zwei hervorragende Schulen, die Architektur- und die Kunsthochschule. Mit den kompetenten Fachleuten vor Ort war es möglich, hochwertige Projekte in großem Maßstab und kurzer Zeit preiswert zu entwickeln und auszuführen. Grundsätzlich sieht der Strategieplan für Saint-Etienne vor, vorhandene Fachkompetenzen zu bündeln (die bautechnischen Dienste des Stadtplanungsamtes unter der Leitung von Alain Cluzet und des Grünflächenamtes unter der Leitung von Christian Réchaussat) und zukünftige Kompetenzen zu

Two important factors helped me in the planning and realisation: on the one hand the strong bond that the residents and technical specialists feel to their city, a popular and very discreet city where ostentatiousness is frowned upon; on the other the two outstanding local schools: the universities of architecture and of art. With competent specialists locally available, it was possible to develop high-quality projects on a large scale in a short time and at low costs.

Basically the strategic plan for Saint-Etienne aims to focus the specialised expertise available (the architectural and construction services of the municipal planning office under the direction of Alain Cluzet and the parks department under Christian Réchaussat) and to develop expertise for the future. To this end we set up a production workshop composed of graduates from the universities. The young architects, designers and artists are to develop designs for the different districts. All of these different specialists are strictly organized, the tasks of each clearly defined and coordinated.

In concrete terms, every year the municipal councillors chose 20 to 30 sites, relatively small but playing an important role in the people's lives, on the basis of their knowledge of the districts and the wishes of the residents. The planning office (under the direction of Jean Paul Seytre) examines the proposals, works out an open space plan and commissions young architects or designers to design the open spaces. The designs are then discussed by the builders, the maintenance services, the government representatives and the residents. They develop and refine the designs together until there is general agreement. Then the urban planning office for green

Um die Stadtflucht zu bremsen, wurde in Saint-Etienne ein Plan zur Quartiersentwicklung aufgelegt. In allen Stadtteilen sollten Plätze aufgewertet werden, die für den Ort oder für die Bewohner wichtig sind. Junge Designer, Künstler und Architekten erarbeiteten Entwürfe in einer Produktionswerkstatt, bei Planung und Realisierung arbeiteten die städtischen Abteilungen eng zusammen. Den Platz Paul-Painlevé (oben) und einen Abschnitt an der Rue Royet gestaltete Hervé Bazile 1998 neu. Die Kosten lagen wie bei allen anderen Projekten sehr niedrig.

In order to stop the exodus from the city, Saint-Etienne established a plan to develop its districts. Sites of importance for the place or the inhabitants were to be upgraded. Young designers, artists and architects developed the designs in a production workshop. The municipal departments carried out the planning and realisation in close co-operation.

Paul-Painlevé Square (top) and part of Royet Street were redesigned by Hervé Bazile in 1998. Costs were very low, as for all the other projects.

areas (director: Francis Alméras) decides whether the projects are technically and financially workable and calls for proposals to execute them. Finally, the same office supervises their realisation along with the young designers. The young planners also participate as free-lance consultants in the Atelier Espaces Publics (Public Space Workshop) where specialists in various fields meet and where all the threads come together. The Marseille designer Charles Bové is the artistic director in the selection process of these young designers.

With the strict organisation and the high quality of the work done by every individual involved, the period of time between the approval and completion of a project is unusually short. This is a great achievement because planning and construction in other cities normally take much longer. Thanks to the participants and organisations named above we are designing about 30 open spaces at the moment. Despite their low budget, formally and in functional value they are of high quality. This is surely proof of the determination of Saint-Etienne's citizens to make large-scale changes in their city on their own and with their own ideas. The place where their plans are devised is the Atelier Espaces Publics, which is also where we create professional expertise on site and probably even a unique Saint-Etienne style.

Some questions by way of a conclusion. In urban design, this discipline without boundaries and without a firmly based profile, I believe it is important to constantly submit what has been completed to critical re-examination. For instance, to what extent should a completed open space project coincide with a preliminary analysis? Are we in danger of creating a new academicism? Sometimes it is a good thing when a design gives a

entwickeln – dazu richteten wir eine Produktionswerkstatt ein, bestehend aus Absolventen der Schulen. Junge Architekten, Designer und Künstler sind mit der Aufgabe betreut, für die verschiedenen Quartiere Entwürfe zu erarbeiten. All diese unterschiedlichen Kompetenzen sind streng organisiert, die Aufgaben eines jeden genau definiert und aufeinander abgestimmt.

Konkret gesprochen sollen die Stadträte jährlich aufgrund ihrer Kenntnis der Wohnviertel und der Wünsche der Einwohner 20 bis 30 relativ kleine Orte auswählen, die eine wichtige Rolle im Leben der Menschen spielen. Das Planungsamt prüft (unter der Leitung Jean Paul Seytres) die Vorschläge, erarbeitet ein Raumprogramm und beauftragt junge Architekten oder Designer mit den Entwürfen der Freiräume. Diese Entwürfe werden wiederum von den Ausführenden, den Pflegebetrieben, den Abgeordneten und den Einwohnern diskutiert. Alle entwickeln und verfeinern sie bis zur Übereinstimmung. Sodann untersucht das städtische Planungsbüro für Grünflächen, geleitet von Francis Alméras, die technische und finanzielle Machbarkeit und schreibt die Projekte aus. Dasselbe Büro überwacht zusammen mit den jungen Entwerfern die Ausführung. Die jungen Planer sind zudem als freischaffende Berater in das sogenannte Atelier Espaces Publics (Werkstatt Öffentlicher Raum) einbezogen, in dem sich die verschiedenen Fachleute treffen und in dem alle Fäden zusammenlaufen. Bei der

Square Visitation/Montaud ist ein schönes Beispiel für eine behutsame Neugestaltung im Sinne des Plans zur Quartiersentwicklung von Saint-Etienne. Rémi Rouchon befreite den Platz vor der Kirche von Montaud von den parkenden Autos und schuf einen würdigen Kirchenvorplatz.

The thoughtful new design for Visitation Square in Montaud is a beautiful example of what Saint-Etienne's plan for district development had in mind. Rémi Rouchon liberated the square from its parked cars and created a worthy square in front of the church of Montaud.

Auswahl der jungen Gestalter übernahm der Marseiller Designer Charles Bové die Rolle des künstlerischen Leiters.

Die strenge Organisation und die Qualität der Arbeit jedes einzelnen ermöglichten es, in außergewöhnlich kurzer Zeit von der Entscheidung zur Fertigstellung eines Projektes zu gelangen. Ein großer Erfolg, denn in anderen Städten dauern Planung und Bau normalerweise viel länger. Dank der genannten Beteiligten und Organisationen gestalten wir momentan jährlich etwa 30 Freiräume, die trotz niedrigen Budgets formal und in ihrem Gebrauchswert hochwertig sind. Sicher ein Beweis für den starken Willen der Saint-Etienner, ihre Stadt aus eigener Kraft und mit eigenen Ideen in großem Maßstab zu verändern. Die Ideenschmiede ist dabei das Atelier Espaces Publics – in ihm formen wir schließlich vor Ort Fachleute, und sicher auch einen eigenen Saint-Etienner Stil.

Einige Fragen als Schlußbetrachtung. In der Stadtgestaltung, dieser Disziplin ohne Grenzen und ohne fest verankertes Profil, scheint es mir wichtig, das Geschaffene fortwährend kritisch zu betrachten. Bis zu welchem Grad sollen die fertigen Freiräume zum Beispiel mit der zuvor erstellten Analyse übereinstimmen? Riskieren wir nicht einen neuen Akademismus? Manchmal tut es gut, wenn Entwürfe einem Raum einen neuen Sinn, eine neue Nutzung bescheren – das Werk von Daniel Buren im Pariser Palais Royal ist in dieser Hinsicht sehr aufschlußreich.

Müssen die Städter wirklich dem verlorenen Landleben nachtrauern? Sollten sie nicht besser zum Städtischen stehen und die städtische Vegetation so gestalten, daß sie nicht zwanghaft das Ländliche nachäfft?

Wenn eine Stadt ein neues repräsentatives Viertel plant und ihre politische oder wirtschaftliche Macht allein durch Bauten in Szene setzt, muß man sich dann nicht fragen, ob unsere Gesellschaft allmählich in akademischem Starrsinn verkrustet? Ohne dem Freiraum mehr Bedeutung beizumessen als er verdient, scheint er mir mehr Facetten der Gesellschaft zu verkörpern als die Bauten: vom römischen Forum als Ort der politischen Auseinandersetzung bis hin zu den großen Plätzen unserer Zeit, auf denen sich alles mögliche ereignet: Feste, Handel, Müßiggang. Wieviele städtische Großprojekte gibt es in Europa, die einmal unter diesem Aspekt betrachtet werden könnten...

Was bedeutet überhaupt »zeitgenössisch gestalten«? Geht es dabei um einen neuen visuellen Ausdruck oder um neue Nutzungen? Freiräume sind heute multifunktional, multikulturell, sogar multiethnisch. Soll die Gestal-

place a new meaning, a new use. Daniel Buren's work in the Parisian Palais Royal is very interesting in this respect.

Do city dwellers really need to mourn the loss of country life? Wouldn't it be better if they were firmly established in urban life and if urban vegetation were designed in a way that did not compulsively imitate the rural?

When a city plans a new representative district and publicizes its political or economic power through buildings alone, shouldn't we be wondering whether our society isn't slowly but surely stultifying in its academic rigidity? Without giving open space more credit than its due, it seems to me that it embodies more facets of society than buildings alone, from the Roman forum as the venue for political discussion up to the large squares of today where all sorts of activities take place: festivals, trade, leisure, events. How many large-scale urban projects in Europe should be subjected to examination from this point of view?

What is modern design really? Is it about new visual expression or new uses? Nowadays open spaces are multifunctional, multicultural and even multiethnic. Should the emphasis be on design or should people's activities be what give spaces their appearance and expression? Compared to the vitality of society, the architects and open space planners sometimes seem more like latecomers than avant-gardists, or even like senile country bumpkins.

Personally, I love Naples because it is a city that unites opposites: beauty and ugliness, easy-goingness and gravity, order and disorder. In short: ambiguity, life itself. My job often requires me to put things in order and give them a place. Or to clear out spaces, according to the principle of subtraction of the Swiss designer Ruedi Baur, which I support. Or to beautify spaces and make them easier to live in. I realise that pioneer days are over, and that we can no longer win battles in design, even temporarily. There is no end in sight for the discourse on urban design, yet I sometimes wish it were over, that we'd achieved what people were hoping for. Which is odd, seeing as how Naples fascinates me while orderly clean cities have no appeal.

What kind of a city are we to build then? The kind that we plan to suit the people we think are so unhappy in their tower blocks? I myself grew up in a village and still remember the smell of old tar, the dilapidated walls, the misshapen huts. A writer who grew up in working-class towns in northern France once told me about her dismay at the way a brilliant and well-meaning architect described the miserable brick housing development that was her home. It was as though it took his words to make her unhappy about her apparently wretched childhood. We should not carry on just because we have the know-how, the way the automobile society is constantly justifying its expansion by its own standards. We should not deprive someone of their memories some day because of what we do.

We should simply know when to stop. The other day I was presented a superb proposal for the new design of a boulevard in an insignificant place in a big city. The borders of the pavements were to measure a grand 50 centimetres and contribute to the project's quality. I suggested that if we reduced the borders from 50 to 30 centimetres we would save a sum that is bigger than that city's cultural budget for its socially challenged districts. Was my objection wrong?

tung überwiegen, oder sollen die Aktivitäten der Menschen erst den Räumen Gestalt und Ausdruck verleihen? Im Vergleich mit der Vitalität der Gesellschaft kommen einem Architekten und Freiraumplaner eher wie ewige Zuspätkommer als wie Avantgardisten vor, vereinzelt gar wie verkalkte Hinterwäldler.

Ich liebe Neapel, denn diese Stadt vereint Gegensätze – das Schöne und das Häßliche, das Leichtlebige und das Schwere, das Aufgeräumte und das Ungeordnete, kurz: das Doppeldeutige, das Leben selbst. Mein Beruf verlangt von mir oft, Dinge zu ordnen und ihnen ihren Platz zuzuweisen. Oder Räume zu entleeren, nach dem Prinzip der Subtraktion des Schweizer Designers Ruedi Baur, das ich unterstütze. Oder Räume zu verschönern und besser nutzbar zu machen. Ich bin mir darüber klar, daß wir heute nicht mehr in Pionierzeiten leben und in der Gestaltung keinen Kampf gewinnen können, nicht einmal vorläufig. Ein Ende der Debatte um die Gestaltung unserer Städte ist nicht abzusehen, und doch sehne ich es manchmal herbei, so wie viele Menschen es vielleicht erwarten. Verwunderlich eigentlich, da mich Neapel fasziniert, und die wohlgeordneten sauberen Städte eher nicht.

Welche Stadt sollen wir also bauen? Diejenige, die wir denen auf den Leib planen, die wir für so unglücklich in ihren Hochhausvierteln halten? Ich bin in einem Dorf aufgewachsen und erinnere mich gut an den Geruch von altem Teer, an verwahrloste Mauern, an häßliche Hütten. Eine Schriftstellerin aus den Arbeiterstädten Nordfrankreichs erzählte mir einmal von ihrer Bestürzung über die Art, wie ein brillanter und wohlwollender Architekt die armselige Backsteinsiedlung ihrer Heimat beschrieb. Es war, als ob erst seine Worte sie darauf gebracht hätten, unglücklich zu sein über ihre angeblich so triste Kindheit. Es geht nicht an, immer wie gehabt weiterzumachen, bloß weil wir das Know-how haben – so wie die Automobilgesellschaft ihre Weiterentwicklung ständig aus sich selbst rechtfertigt. Es geht nicht an, daß irgendwann jemand durch unser Tun seine Erinnerungen verliert. Wir sollten einfach wissen, wann wir aufhören müssen.

Neulich wurde mir ein wunderbarer Entwurf vorgelegt für die Neugestaltung eines Boulevards an einem bedeutungslosen Ort einer Großstadt. Die Gehwegeinfassungen sollten luxuriöse 50 Zentimeter messen und den Wert des Projekts steigern. Ich gab folgendes zu bedenken: Wenn wir die Einfassungen von 50 auf 30 Zentimeter reduzieren, sparen wir eine Summe, die größer ist als das Kulturbudget der betreffenden Großstadt für die sozial schwachen Viertel. Ist mein Einwand falsch?

Der öffentliche Raum als Ware

Public space: goods for sale

Bruno Flierl

Die dem Allgemeingebrauch gewidmeten, offen zugänglichen und in diesem Sinne öffentlichen Räume der Stadt – Straßen, Plätze und Parkanlagen – sind schon seit langem nicht mehr das, was sie einmal waren oder sein sollten, nämlich Räume einer Stadtgesellschaft, die ihre eigene Öffentlichkeit wie ihre eigene Individualität braucht, schafft und garantiert. Diese Stadtgesellschaft, die eben dadurch lebt, dass sich ihre Mitglieder auch im öffentlichen Raum – wie übereinstimmend oder widersprüchlich auch immer – in ihren Interessen an der sie alle verbindenden öffentlichen Sache, der res publica, artikulieren und vermitteln, verschwindet zunehmend, nicht nur deshalb, weil personale Kommunikation in städtischen Räumen durch Tele-Kommunikation mehr und mehr ersetzt wird, sondern weil an die Stelle gesellschaftlicher Interessen marktwirtschaftliche Interessen – und das sind in erster Linie private ökonomische Interessen – Leben und Raum der Stadt bestimmen und deren gesellschaftliche Potenz aushöhlen. Je dominanter Privatisierung und Vermarktung voranschreiten, desto mehr verdrängen und ersetzen sie die gesellschaftlichen Anlässe, Formen und Wirkungen bisheriger Begegnungen einzelner Menschen und sozialer Gruppen im offen zugänglichen Raum der Stadt – bei kulturellen Veranstaltungen wie bei politischen Demonstrationen. Von gesellschaftlichen Ursachen und Wirkungen entfremdete Begegnungen aber werden zu Begegnungen von Fremden. Hinzu kommt, dass mehr und mehr die privaten Eigner bestimmen, was auf ihrem Grund und Boden bis zur Größe ganzer Stadtviertel zur Belebung ihrer Geschäfte und ihres Rufes an Leben und Erleben – Events, wie es jetzt heißt – inszeniert wird und was auf den von ihnen kontrollierten Flächen der Stadt nicht stattfinden darf. Und ebenso inszenieren private Veranstalter in zeitweilig angemieteten öffentlichen Räumen städtischen Eigentums Events nach ihrem Gusto und machen sie über die unmittelbar Beteiligten hinaus auf dem Wege über angeheuerte private Medien des Fernsehens und des Funks zum Mega-Event für die ganze Stadt, für das ganze Land und womöglich für die ganze Welt. Daran verdienen alle Produzenten und Promoteure: die Veranstalter, die Medien und die in public-private-partnership angeschlossenen Stadtverwaltungen, die selbst finanziell zu arm und kulturell zu einfallslos sind, ihren Bürgern städtische Erlebnisse zu schaffen.

Ökonomie sticht Gesellschaft: In Berlin wird der öffentliche Raum zunehmend nach marktwirtschaftlichen Interessen gestaltet.

Economics wins against society: Berlin's public space is being shaped more and more by economic interests.

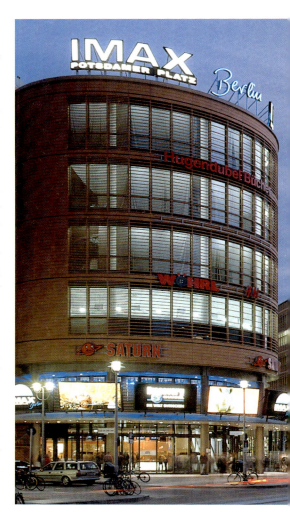

Streets, squares and parks dedicated to public use, freely accessible and hence the public spaces of the city, have not been what they once were or should be for a long time. They should be places for an urban society that requires and creates and guarantees both its public aspect and its individ-

Showpiece project on Potsdamer Platz: the Daimler Chrysler buildings with Marlene Dietrich Square, and the debis head office (in the centre) by Renzo Piano and Christoph Kohlbecker. The redistribution of land according to economic considerations reflects the powers that be: in public space, economic interests predominate. The original plan was for a compact piece of a typical European city, with streets and squares.

uality. This urban society lives on the fact that its members can express themselves and communicate their interests in common public affairs, regardless of how harmoniously or contradictorily, in public space. This urban society is gradually disappearing not only because personal communication in urban spaces is increasingly being replaced by telecommunication but also because economic interests, primarily private, instead of social ones are determining the life and the spaces in the city and undermining their social potential. The more privatisation and marketing pre-

Vorzeigeprojekt auf dem Potsdamer Platz: das Daimler Chrysler-Areal mit dem Marlene-Dietrich-Platz, in der Bildmitte der debis-Firmensitz von Renzo Piano und Christoph Kohlbecker. Die Neuverteilung der Grundstücke nach wirtschaftlichen Aspekten spiegelt Herrschaftspositionen: Ökonomische Interessen dominieren den öffentlichen Raum. Geplant war ein Stück kompakte europäische Stadt mit Straßen und Plätzen.

Inszenierte Events im öffentlichen Raum, das ist die Ware, die verkauft wird – am wirkungsvollsten in den historischen Kulissen der Stadt. Dabei bleibt die Stadt nicht nur Hülle und Verpackung der Ware Event, sondern wird selbst zur Ware, die da verkauft wird. Berlin bietet dafür zwei besonders anschauliche Beispiele: am Potsdamer Platz und entlang der großen Stadtachse östlich und westlich des Brandenburger Tores, beide bedeutende historische städtebauliche Bereiche, die durch die Spaltung der Stadt ihrer ehemals Ost und West verbindenden Funktion beraubt waren und diese nun wieder herzustellen suchen – praktisch im Leben der Stadt und symbolisch im Sinne deutscher Vereinigung.

Der neue Potsdamer Platz: eine City als Themenpark. Was heute Potsdamer Platz genannt wird, ist ein Stadtgebiet, das vom Verkehrsknotenpunkt Potsdamer Platz als Straßenkreuzung und als Station des Schienenverkehrs bis zum Kulturforum reicht. Dieses Stadtgebiet kauften und gestalteten zwei private Mega-Investoren als Developer – Daimler und Sony – sowohl zum eigenen Gebrauch als auch zur Vermarktung an fremde Nutzer mit Raum für Büroarbeit und Wohnen, für exquisite Gaststätten und Geschäfte, für ein Luxushotel sowie für Einrichtungen der Kultur und Unterhaltung mit Groß-Kinos, Musical-Theater und Spielcasino, aber auch zur Inszenierung von Events im offen zugänglichen Außenraum, den sie durch eine eigene Polizei vor Missbrauch bewachen lassen, und der deshalb kein eigentlich öffentlicher Raum ist.

Laut Planungsabsicht – anfangs noch im Konsens beider Investoren und der Stadtplanung – sollte das Daimler-Center, inzwischen Center der Daimler Chrysler Corporation, ein Stück kompakte europäische Stadt mit Straßen und Plätzen werden, das Sony-Center dagegen ein Stück kompakte Stadt mit einer zentralen Mall nach amerikanischem Vorbild. Aber entgegen den ursprünglichen Absprachen setzte Daimler in vorauseilender Konkurrenz zu Sony statt einer offenen Geschäftsstraße eine glasüberdachte Straßenmall durch, die so genannten Potsdamer Platz Arkaden. Als öffentlicher Außenraum verblieben im wesentlichen die wieder verlebendigte alte Potsdamer Straße mit dem neu angelegten Marlene-Dietrich-Platz, der sie allerdings auch beendet, da das hinter dem Musical-Theater und dem Spielcasino und parallel zu ihnen liegende Gebäude der Staatsbibliothek im Kulturforum einer Weiterführung der Straße wie eine Barriere im Wege steht. Diese so verkürzte alte Potsdamer Straße von insgesamt etwas mehr als 200 Meter Länge als Rückgrat des öffentlichen Raumes eines pri-

dominate, the more they will crowd out and replace the social opportunities, forms and results of the customary encounters among individuals and social groups in freely accessible spaces in the city – at both cultural events and political demonstrations. Encounters estranged from social causes and effects become encounters between strangers. Moreover, private owners are more and more often calling the shots on what should be staged on their property, which may be as big as an entire city district. These events, as they are called nowadays, aim to enhance the owners' businesses and reputations. Of course the owners also decide what is not allowed to take place on the urban land they control. Similarly, private organisers can stage whatever they like on temporarily rented public pieces of municipal property. They hire private media, television and radio, and make the event above and beyond the parties directly involved into a mega-event for the whole city, for the whole country and if possible for the whole world. All of the producers and promoters profit: the organisers, the media and the municipal administrations in the so-called public-private partnership, who are themselves too poor and too unimaginative in matters of culture to create urban experiences for their residents.

Organised events in public space are the goods that are being sold. They are most effective against the city's historical backdrops. That means the city is not only the packaging of the event 'goods' but also becomes itself the goods that are being sold. Berlin provides two especially good examples of this trend, one at Potsdamer Platz and the other along the big axis of the city east and west of the Brandenburger Tor (Brandenburg Gate). Both are important, historical, urbanistic features robbed through the division of the city of their former function as east-west links. They are now trying to revive this function, both in practical terms in the life of the city and symbolically in the sense of German unification.

The new Potsdamer Platz: downtown as a theme park. What is called Potsdamer Platz today is a city district that extends from the Potsdamer Platz traffic junction to the Kulturforum in the form of an intersection and a station for rail traffic. This city district was purchased and shaped by two private mega-investors functioning as developers: Daimler and Sony. It was built both for being used by them and marketed to outside users. There is room for offices and housing, exquisite restaurants and shops and a luxury hotel as well as facilities for culture and entertainment with large cinemas, a musical theatre and a casino. There is also room for events to be held in the freely accessible open space, which the owners have guarded against misuse with a police force of their own and which is therefore not really a public space.

Still with the consensus of both investors and the municipal planning office at first, planning intended the Daimler Centre, now the Centre of the Daimler Chrysler Corporation, to become a compact piece of European-style city. It was to have streets and squares. The Sony Centre, on the other hand, was to be a compact piece of city with a central mall along American lines. Contrary to the original agreements, however, Daimler hurried on ahead in competition with Sony and came through with, instead of an open shopping street, a street mall with a glass roof, the so-called Potsdamer Platz Arcades. All that was left as public outdoor space is basically the revitalised

vaten Stadtgebiets rechtfertigt nicht, von europäischer Stadt und schon gar nicht von »Daimler-City« und von »neuer Mitte« in Berlin zu sprechen, wie das die Werbung tut.

Heute – gut drei Jahre nach der Öffnung der Potsdamer Platz Arkaden in der Daimler City und zwei Jahre nach der Einweihung des Sony Centers – kann jeder selbst sehen, was beide Bereiche mit ihrer gepriesenen Faszination der Mitte wert sind, und wie sie als öffentlicher Raum und damit als Raum von Öffentlichkeit funktionieren. Das Ergebnis ist widersprüchlich. Auf der einen Seite ist dieses neue Stück Stadt überaus stark besucht, es wird ganz offensichtlich zunächst einmal angenommen. Das ist nicht nur der nach wie vor anhaltenden Propaganda und den Aktivitäten des Tourismus zu verdanken, sondern ganz einfach auch der Tatsache, dass Stadtbewohner wie Stadtbesucher stets auf der Suche nach Neuem sind, besonders nach der Erfüllung verkündeter Träume. »Muss ich sehen!« So lautet wie in einem bekannten privaten Fernsehsender die Motivation. Aber dann – oft erst beim zweiten Blick – wird auch die inhaltliche Leere der offen zugänglichen Außenräume bemerkt, ihre fehlende urbane Öffentlichkeit, die durch Kaufangebote mit Erlebnis-Charakter und gelegentlich inszenierte Events nicht ersetzt werden kann.

Und schließlich wird nicht übersehen, dass das ganze neue Stadtgebiet natürlich keine neue Mitte von Berlin ist, sondern eine in der Mitte von Berlin gebaute Insel, die ringsum mit der Stadt weder funktionell noch räumlich aktiv verbunden ist: Sie liegt Rücken an Rücken zum Kulturforum, ohne lebendige öffentliche Verbindung zur Potsdamer Straße in Schöneberg und zur Friedrichstraße im Bezirk Mitte, aber auch verloren zwischen dem Diplomatenviertel südlich des Tiergartens und dem Regierungsviertel nördlich davon. Sie ist kein Ort auf den Wegen zwischen diesen Bereichen, sondern ein Punkt zwischen ihnen. Dieser Ort könnte auch woanders liegen in der Stadt. Und eben deshalb ist er keine neue Stadtmitte.

Gedacht war der Potsdamer Platz – ganz nach dem Vorbild von Disneyland – als ein Themenpark. Das Thema lautete Stadt und City. Aber er ist nicht real, sondern nur virtuell Stadt und City. Und das genügt nicht. Anders als die Amerikaner akzeptieren die Europäer solche virtuellen Stadtinszenierungen von Paris und Venedig wie in Las Vegas bislang noch nicht als Realität. Wie lange noch?

Die alte historische Stadtachse: eine Festmeile für Hauptstadtparties. Auf

Der Sony-Gebäudekomplex, Exempel für die Gesellschaft. Die Investoren benutzen den öffentlichen Raum zur Selbstdarstellung und zur Vermarktung an andere Nutzer. Die öffentlichen Räume sind den Menschen nicht wirklich öffentlich zugänglich. Die »neue Mitte«, bloßer Werbeslogan, gar ein Ort der Simulation?

The Sony group of buildings is an image of our society. The investors use the public space to promote themselves and to market it to other users. The public spaces are not really open to the public. Is the "new centre of Berlin" only a commercial slogan or even a mere simulation?

Die Potsdamer Platz Arkaden. Was als zentrale Mall nach amerikanischem Vorbild geplant war, nämlich eine offene Geschäftsstraße, mutierte zu einer glasüberdachten Einkaufszone. Kommerz ersetzt die fehlende urbane Öffentlichkeit.

The Potsdamer Platz Arcades: the central mall planned along American lines as an open street with shops has metamorphosed into a shopping area under a glass roof. Commercialism takes the place of lacking urban public life.

23

Old Potsdamer Street and the newly set up Marlene Dietrich Square. It ends there, for the State Library building in the Kulturforum behind the musical theatre and the casino parallel to them is like a barrier blocking the continuation of the street. The thus shortened Old Potsdamer Street, the inner backbone a little over 200 metres long of the public space of a private city district, does not justify talk of a European city and especially not of Daimler City or the "new city centre of Berlin" as in the advertisements.

Today, a good three years after the opening of the Potsdamer Platz Arcades in Daimler City and nearly two yaers after the inauguration of the

Sony Centre, anyone can see for themselves what the two areas are worth with their celebrated "downtown fascination" and how they work as public space and thus as space for public life. The result is contradictory. On the one hand this new piece of city has very many visitors; for the time being it is obviously being accepted. This is due not only to continuing propaganda and tourism but also to the simple fact that city dwellers and city visitors are always on the lookout for something new, especially for predicted dreams come true. "I've got to see it!" is what motivates them, as the slogan of a well-known private television station puts it. Later, often only after a second look, they notice the lack of content in these freely accessible outdoor spaces, the lack of an urban public aspect. It cannot be replaced by sales offers with adventure elements and by occasionally staged events. Finally, they cannot overlook the fact that the whole new city district is of course not a centre of Berlin but an island built in the centre of Berlin, actively linked in neither functional nor spatial terms with the city around it. Back to back to the Kulturforum without a live public connection to Potsdamer Street in Schöneberg or Friedrich Street in Mitte, it is also lost between the diplomatic district south of Tiergarten and the government district north of Tiergarten. It is not a place on the way to these areas but a spot between them. It could be anywhere else in the city. That is why it is not a new city centre.

Potsdamer Platz was conceived, fully along the lines of Disneyland, as a theme park. Its theme was city and downtown. But it is not a real city and downtown, only a virtual one. And that is not enough. Unlike Americans, Europeans cannot yet accept the staging of a virtual city as reality, such as Paris and Venice in Las Vegas. But for how long yet?

The historic urban axis: a festive mile for parties in the capital. Marketing the central part of the major historic east-west axis of Berlin as public space is happening in a different way from that at Potsdamer Platz. It only concerns the purchase of rights for private use, not the purchase of property for it. Ever since the wall came down, marketing for tourism along this great axis between Grosser Stern with its Siegessäule and Rotes Rathaus has always focused on Pariser Platz with the Brandenburg Gate. The only exceptions are the monument to Soviet heroes and the Palast der Republik as mementoes of the lost World War II and the GDR era.

From the start the Berlin Senate Administration had relatively unclear ideas for the urban function and hence the public use of Pariser Platz. At least it did not turn the square into Berlin's "presentable sitting room" the way Senator Nagel would have liked. At first the square was actually a souvenir market, with strong support from the Senate, activated by tourism. The spoils for sale were GDR army emblems and Russian hats. It later became more and more of a venue for re-unification parties to commemorate the fall of the wall and for national festivities in the capital, with stages for orchestras and singers, market stalls, and the ever present huge crowds. It was the central place for establishing festivals in the capital. Its sign and prize, the Brandenburg Gate was marketed as a national symbol and a focus of publicity.

All perceptive planners are aware that Pariser Platz is not suited for events of this kind at all.

andere Art als am Potsdamer Platz vollzieht sich die Vermarktung des zentral gelegenen Teils der großen historischen Ost-West Stadtachse von Berlin als öffentlicher Raum. Hier geht es allein um den Kauf von Rechten zur privaten Nutzung, nicht auch um den Kauf von Grund und Boden dafür. Zentraler Punkt touristischer Vermarktung entlang dieser großen Achse im Bereich zwischen dem Großen Stern mit der Siegessäule und dem Roten Rathaus war seit dem Fall der Mauer immer wieder vor allem der Pariser Platz mit dem Brandenburger Tor. Ausgeklammert blieben das Sowjetische Ehrenmal und der Palast der Republik als Erinnerungsstücke an den verlorenen Zweiten Weltkrieg und an die Zeit der DDR.

Über die städtische Funktion und damit auch öffentliche Nutzung des Pariser Platzes gab es seitens der Senatsverwaltung von Anfang an relativ unklare Vorstellungen. Zur »guten Stube« Berlins, wie Senator Nagel dies wollte, ist er jedenfalls nicht geworden. Was der Platz – mit kräftiger Unterstützung des Senats – tatsächlich wurde, das war zuerst ein touristisch aktivierter Andenkenmarkt mit Beutegut – NVA-Embleme und Russen-Mützen – und dann zunehmend ein Ort für Einheitsfeiern zur Erinnerung an den Mauerfall und für nationale Hauptstadtfeste mit Bühnen für Orchester, Sänger und Schausteller und immer riesigem Massenandrang, ein zentraler Ort der Hauptstadt-Festivalisierung, zu deren Zeichen und Auszeichnung das Brandenburger Tor als nationales Symbol und als Fokus von Öffentlichkeit vermarktet wurde.

Allen einsichtigen Planern ist bewusst, dass der Pariser Platz für Veranstaltungen dieser Art im Grunde überhaupt nicht geeignet ist, weder ideell von seiner Funktion und Bedeutung im Leben und Raum der Stadt, noch praktisch von seiner Verwendbarkeit für die Ansammlung großer Massen, ganz abgesehen von seiner Erreichbarkeit und Sicherheit. Er wird es künftig immer weniger sein, sobald die noch nicht gebauten Botschaften der USA und Frankreichs errichtet und bewacht sein werden. Trotzdem haben Staat und Stadt kein konstruktives Konzept, dem offensichtlichen Bedürf-

Noch 1995 hielten sich am Pariser Platz die Andenkenverkäufer auf. Am Potsdamer Platz sammelt sich dagegen heute das Kapital. »Mehr Demokratie!« forderte einst Willy Brandt für die alte Bundesrepublik. Sollten nicht heute gesamtgesellschaftliche Interessen über Privatinteressen gesetzt werden? Und sollte nicht der öffentliche Raum von demokratischen gesinnten Menschen auch politisch genutzt werden?

Until 1995, Pariser Platz was still full of souvenir vendors. Potsdamer Platz on the other hand, is amassing capital. "More democracy!" was once Willy Brandt's appeal to the old Federal Republic of Germany. Shouldn't the interests of the society as a whole have precedence over private ones today? And shouldn't public space also be used for political purposes by democratically minded people?

There is neither an ideological basis of function and meaning in the life and space of the city, nor a practical one of suitability for assembling huge crowds, not to mention accessibility and security. The latter will be even less the case in future once the embassies of the USA and France are built and under guard. Nevertheless, the state and the city have no constructive concept to satisfy the population's obvious need for public space for urban life and for festivities in the centre of town. Could it be that because the state and the city lack not only money but also a positive concept for the people as citizens in the city's public space, they are better off leaving the public space to private enterprise to market for popular events without social (to say nothing of political) content? What this could mean for the future was demonstrated in exemplary fashion at New Year's Eve 1999-2000.

The millennium celebration organised by a private company "Silvester in Berlin GmbH" (New Year's Eve in Berlin Co.) headed by Willy Kausch and entailing a great expense – 40 million germanmarks – was to be the greatest party in the capital of all times. And it was. Kausch decreed the over four-kilometre-long central part of the urban axis from Grosser Stern through Pariser Platz to the square in front of the Rotes Rathaus as a festival mile, and the Siegessäule and Brandenburg Gate along it as the focal points of the event. The entire stretch was equipped with stages and podiums for musical events and broadcasting stations for radio and television. Stages on either side of the Brandenburg Gate, however, prevented people from walking through the gate, counteracting the significance of the gates on this night of all nights of the millennium

Ausgestrahlte Lichtshow in der Silversternacht 1999/2000. Das ursprüngliche Konzept von »art in heaven« wurde nach öffentlicher Diskussion wegen zu großer Ähnlichkeit zu den Lichtdomen Albert Speers verworfen.

Beams of the light show on New Year's Eve 1999-2000. The original idea of "art in heaven" was dropped was dropped after public debate for being too close to Albert speer's light domes.

nis der Bevölkerung nach öffentlichem Raum für urbanes Leben und für Festivitäten mitten in der Stadt Rechnung zu tragen. Sollte es zutreffen, dass Staat und Stadt nicht nur aus Geldmangel, sondern weil sie kein positives Konzept für den Bürger als Citoyen im öffentlichen Raum der Stadt besitzen, besser privaten Nutzern und Veranstaltern den öffentlichen Raum für publikumsattraktive Events ohne gesellschaftlichen oder gar politischen Inhalt zur Vermarktung überlassen? Was dies für die Zukunft bedeuten würde, zeigte sich zu Silvester 1999/2000 geradezu modellhaft.

Die von der privaten »Silvester in Berlin GmbH« unter Leitung von Willy Kausch mit großem Aufwand – 40 Millionen Mark – vorbereitete Millenniumsfeier sollte die größte Hauptstadtparty aller Zeiten werden. Und das wurde sie denn auch. Kausch bestimmte den über vier Kilometer langen mittleren Teil der Stadtachse vom Großen Stern über den Pariser Platz bis zum Platz vor dem Roten Rathaus zur Festmeile und darin die Siegessäule und das Brandenburger Tor zu Brennpunkten des Events. Die gesamte Strecke war mit Bühnen und Podien für musikalische Veranstaltungen und Übertragungsstationen für Funk und Fernsehen ausgestattet. Bühnen zu beiden Seiten des Brandenburger Tors verhinderten jedoch das Durchschreiten des Tores und konterkarierten damit seine Bedeutung gerade in dieser Nacht der Millenniumsfeier: Einerseits war das Brandenburger Tor Symbol deutscher Einheit – wie es seit dem Fall der Mauer 1989 ständig im Bewusstsein gehalten wird – über die Medien in aller Welt virtuell präsent, selbst aber zwischen den Bezirken Tiergarten und Mitte geschlossen, also real nicht passierbar. Was für eine Botschaft für alle, die in dieser Nacht am Brandenburger Tor – westlich und östlich voneinander getrennt – feierten!

Am Rande dieser Festmeile als öffentlicher Stadtraum waren nichtöffentliche Parties für VIP-Teilnehmer der Silvesternacht in nichtöffentlichen Innenräumen arrangiert: in der Staatsoper Unter den Linden, im Hotel Adlon und in der Dresdner Bank am Pariser Platz, in der Kuppel und auf der Dachterrasse des Reichstagsgebäudes sowie in Gala-Zelten rings um dieses Gebäude.

Das ergab ein zutreffendes sozial-räumliches Abbild von Öffentlichkeit: draußen auf den Straßen und Plätzen und im Tiergarten das Volk, drinnen in den repräsentativen Gebäuden am Rande der Festmeile die Crème der Gesellschaft. Für alle gemeinsam war eine Mega-Lightshow an der Siegessäule und ein Riesenfeuerwerk am Brandenburger Tor vorgesehen, die sie

celebration. On the one hand the Brandenburg Gate as the symbol of German unity, constantly being kept in our awareness since the fall of the wall in 1989, was virtually present through the media all over the world. On the other, as a gate between the Tiergarten and Mitte districts, it was closed, that is not passable in reality. What a message for everyone celebrating at the Brandenburg Gate that night – separated eastwards and westwards from each other!

On the edges of this festive mile on public urban space, non-public parties were held for VIP guests in non-public indoor spaces. These were in the Staatsoper Unter den Linden (state opera house), in Hotel Adlon and in the Dresdner Bank on Pariser Platz, in the dome and on the roof terrace of the Reichstag as well as in gala tents around the building.

The result was a fitting picture of public life in social and spatial terms: outside on the streets and squares and in Tiergarten were the people, inside in the representative buildings on the edge of the festival mile was the social élite of society. Intended for all of them together, a mega light show at the Siegessäule and gigantic fireworks at the Brandenburg Gates were to illuminate them all under the sky of Berlin. This was a flop because an unusually low fog over the city and the billowing smoke from the fireworks swallowed up the light beams. Nevertheless, the merriment of the millennium New Year's Eve party was not much affected.

As reported live by the media, the public celebrated at a party that was like the fall of the wall and the Love Parade in one. Surely it was more the Love Parade tradition that had come to the fore. At the exclusive parties in sheltered indoor

Auf Deutsch zuerst erschienen im Jahrbuch 2000 »Architektur in Berlin«. Herausgeber Architektenkammer Berlin. Junius-Verlag, Hamburg.

First published in German in the 2000 yearbook, "Architektur in Berlin" of the Architektenkammer Berlin by Junius Publishers, Hamburg.

venues on the edge of the street, the others were celebrating at the same time at one thousand marks and up for admission. Outside in the city's public space, mostly complete strangers were hugging and kissing at midnight, as the media delightedly reported. The ladies and gentlemen toasting each other indoors in the non-public spaces all knew each other: as public personalities of the city and the state.

The last act of the millennium party was played by the municipal street-cleaners. Two million partygoers – those out there! – produced a total of 200 tons of refuse in the city's public space. Nevertheless, because it was all so much fun and almost no trouble at all for the police and the fire brigade, but especially because it was economically so successful for the private organisers and the private media allied with them, the party is not over. The fun is to go on because, as the press concluded, Berlin has become the party capital of Germany and is supposed to remain so in future.

Does that mean continuing in the same familiar way? Or should social interests in using the city's public space not be placed above private interests after all? That would mean to consider and practise public-private partnership in general, and in this case in particular, no longer primarily in terms of private economic interests but comprehensively oriented to the public and society. Why should festivals and events not enliven the city's public space more often without predominant private marketing, especially along the great urban axis of Berlin, as on Blade Nights? Last but not least, why should democratically minded people not use the public space of the city, particularly of their capital city, for demonstrating, e.g. against right-wing extremism?

alle unter dem Himmel von Berlin erleuchten sollte. Diese aber schlug fehl, weil die ausgestrahlten Lichter von einem außergewöhnlich tiefhängenden Nebel über der Stadt wie auch von den Rauchschwaden des Feuerwerks verschluckt wurden. Das jedoch störte die Ausgelassenheit der Millenniums-Silvesterparty im Grunde nicht.

Das Volk feierte – wie die Medien live berichteten – die Party wie Mauerfall und Love Parade in einem. Freilich war es doch wohl mehr die Tradition der Love Parade, die da durchschlug. In den exklusiven Parties in geschützten Innenräumen am Straßenrand feierten zur gleichen Zeit die anderen für Eintrittsgelder ab tausend Mark aufwärts. Draußen im öffentlichen Raum der Stadt umarmten und küssten sich um Mitternacht zumeist gänzlich Unbekannte, wie die Medien – davon selbst entzückt – berichteten. Die Damen und Herren, die sich innen in den nichtöffentlichen Räumen zuprosteten, kannten sich alle: als Persönlichkeiten des öffentlichen Lebens der Stadt und des Staates.

Den letzten Akt der Millenniumsparty vollzog dann die Stadtreinigung. Zwei Millionen Partyteilnehmer – die da draußen! – hatten im öffentlichen Raum der Stadt insgesamt 200 Tonnen Müll produziert. Und trotzdem: Weil alles so schön war und für die Polizei und Feuerwehr der Stadt fast problemlos, vor allem aber auch ökonomisch so effektiv für die privaten Veranstalter und die mit ihnen verbündeten privaten Medien, soll es in Zukunft so weitergehen, denn, so wurde von der Presse resümiert: Berlin ist zur Party-Hauptstadt Deutschlands geworden – und soll es auch bleiben.

Also: weiter so nach dem eingeübten Modell? Oder sollte nicht doch das gesellschaftliche Interesse über das private Interesse an der Nutzung des öffentlichen Raumes in der Stadt gesetzt werden? Das aber hieße, public-private-partnership generell und in diesem Falle speziell nicht weiterhin primär privat-marktwirtschaftlich, sondern übergreifend öffentlich-gesellschaftlich zu denken und zu praktizieren. Warum sollten nicht viel öfter Feste und Events jenseits dominanter privater Vermarktung den öffentlichen Raum der Stadt, gerade auch entlang der großen Stadtachse Berlins, beleben – wie die Blade-Nights? Und warum sollte ein demokratisch gesinntes Volk den öffentlichen Raum der Stadt, gerade der Hauptstadt, nicht auch politisch nutzen, nicht zuletzt, wenn es darum geht, gegen Rechts zu demonstrieren?

Eine Uferpromenade ohne Ufer in Barcelona

A riverbank promenade without a riverbank in Barcelona

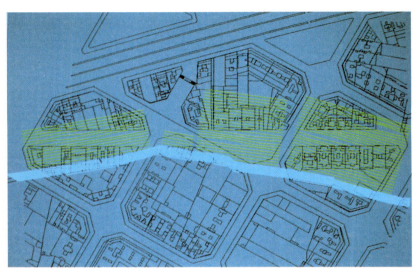 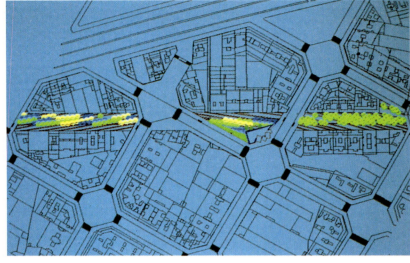

Andreu Arriola
Carmen Fiol

Am Anfang des Entwerfens steht für uns immer die Annäherung an den Ort. Aus dem Ort selbst entsteht das Projekt – er ist nicht nur die Kulisse, die den Entwurf einschränkt und behindert. In der Analyse des Ortes decken wir die Regeln auf, die den Entwurf bestimmen, sei es für den öffentlichen Raum, für ein Gebäude oder für einen ganzen Stadtteil mit Gebäuden und Freiräumen. Und mehr: Durch unsere Arbeit in der Stadt von heute haben wir erfahren, daß die Dualität von bebautem und unbebautem Raum sich auflöst in einer gemeinsamen Organisation.

Der erste Besuch eines Ortes bedeutet uns viel. Da erleben wir seine Atmosphäre mit allen Sinnen. Nicht nur die Architektur des Ortes wird uns klar, sondern auch seine anderen Merkmale: wie er genutzt wird, welche Punkte, Linien und Niveaus sich aus der Nutzung ergeben, der Autoverkehr, die Ein- und Ausgänge zu Tiefgaragen und U-Bahn, Markt, Schule, Geschäfte, die Wege der Fußgänger, Veranstaltungen im Freien, Versammlungsorte. Besonders fällt uns auf, was die Sinne anspricht: die Geräuschkulisse, die Besonnung, Wind, Vegetation. Gleichzeitig betrachten wir die Umgebung des Ortes: seine Topographie, den Straßenverlauf,

Ein unterirdischer Kanal bestimmt das neue Design der Calle Bofarull. Höhepunkt ist ein skulpturaler Platz mit künstlichem Geysir.
A subterranean canal determines the new design of the Calle Bofarull. It culminates in a sculptural square with an artificial geyser.

For us the beginning of a design always consists of getting to know a place. The project evolves from the place itself, which is not merely the backdrop, limiting and hindering the design. In our analysis of a place we uncover guidelines determining the design, whether it be for a public place, for a building, or for a whole part of town with buildings and open spaces. Furthermore, by working in today's city we have discovered that the duality of built-up and undeveloped space dissolves in one common organisation.

Our first visit to a place is very significant. We experience its atmosphere with all our senses. Not only the architecture of the place becomes clear to us, but also its other distinguishing features: how it is used, which points, lines and levels evolve from its uses, the automobile traffic, the entries and exits of subterranean parking and the underground, the market, school, shops, pedestrian routes, open-air events, and gathering

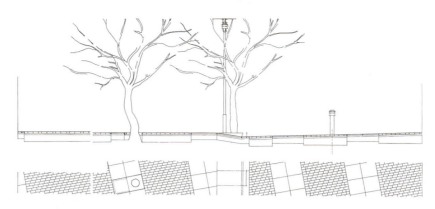

places. We especially notice what addresses the senses: the background noise, sunlight, wind and vegetation. We also observe the surroundings of the place: its topography, the course of the streets, the height of the buildings, their density, the size of the lots and their orientation, and the gaps between them. After making these observations we decide which features we would like to emphasize in the design and which to tone down in order to lend the place character. We also collect historical information. With the help of city maps, photographs and literary descriptions we find out how the city of today developed as the result of many different interventions in the course of time. We merely add another one and thus further rotate the wheel of history.

We would like to create contemporary spaces. This aim is expressed in our disposition of the spaces, our architectural vocabulary, in the details and the new materials. We design with intuition and feeling, and with as little material and expenditure as possible. This minimalism rationalizes and simplifies the design, making it sensitive and convincing.

Our construction materials are almost always traditional: brick, travertine, wood, metal, and glass. Yet we use them in an unusual way. We combine various textures and colours, shiny and dull surfaces, in an utterly unclassical manner. In public spaces we like to experiment with new materials that are especially resistant and need little maintenance: Corten steel, combinations of Corten steel and wood, and high-grade steel. Every detail is carried out such that the idea of the design is recognizable within it.

The Calle Bofarull and Plaça d'Islandia design is to reveal typical elements of the new sub-

Der Kanal Rec Comptal und die alte Calle Bofarull bestimmten einst den Grundriß des Stadtviertels Navas. Heute verläuft der Kanal unterirdisch und die Stadt ist durch das Schachbrettmuster des Ensanche Cerdá geprägt (gegenüber). Um den Kanal formal wieder ans Licht zu holen, übertragen Tangenten seine Biegung auf die Calle Bofarull. Darauf pflanzten die Planer Bäume und gestalteten ein neues Pflaster.

The Rec Comptal canal and Calle Bofarull determine the layout of the district of Navas. The canal runs underground today and the city is characterized by the checkerboard Ensanche Cerdá grid (opposite). To bring the canal formally to light again, tangents of its curves were transposed onto the Calle Bofarull. The planners planted trees on it and designed a new pavement.

die Gebäudehöhen, ihre Dichte, die Parzellengrößen und -ausrichtung, die Durchblicke. Nach dieser Betrachtung entscheiden wir, welche Eigenschaften des Ortes wir im Entwurf verstärken und welche wir abschwächen möchten, um ihm Charakter zu verleihen. Auch über die Geschichte des Ortes machen wir uns kundig. Anhand von Stadtplänen, Fotografien und Literatur finden wir heraus, wie sich die Stadt entwickelt hat – ein Produkt vieler verschiedener Eingriffe im Laufe der Zeit. Wir fügen lediglich einen hinzu und drehen so das Rad der Geschichte ein Stück weiter.

Wir möchten zeitgenössische Räume schaffen. Dieses Anliegen drückt sich aus in der Organisation unserer Räume, im architektonischen Vokabular, in den Details und den neuen Materialien. Wir entwerfen mit Intuition und Gefühl und mit möglichst wenig Material und Aufwand. Dieser Minimalismus rationalisiert und vereinfacht den Entwurf, macht ihn sensibel und überzeugend. Unsere Baumaterialien sind fast immer traditionell: Ziegelstein, Travertin, Holz, Metall, Glas. Aber wir verwenden sie auf ungewohnte Weise. Unterschiedliche Texturen und Farben, glänzende und stumpfe Oberflächen fügen wir ganz unklassisch zusammen. Im öffentlichen Raum experimentieren wir gerne mit neuen Materialien, die besonders widerstandsfähig sind und wenig Pflege bedürfen: Corten-Stahl, Kombinationen aus Corten-Stahl und Holz, Edelstahl. Jedes Detail führen wir so aus, daß man darin die Idee des Entwurfs wiedererkennt.

Im Design der Calle Bofarull und der Plaça d'Islandia soll sich das Typische der neuen Vorstadt zeigen: die Leere zwischen den Bauten, das Negativ zur Architektur. Wir organisierten den Raum so, daß er offen und dynamisch wirkt. Einfache euklidische Körper ordneten wir scheinbar willkürlich auf dem Platz an. In Wirklichkeit nehmen sie Linien und Richtungen auf, die wir aus dem Stadtgrundriß ableiteten. So bietet sich den Spaziergängern von verschiedenen Standpunkten immer wieder ein neues Bild. Diese Verankerung im Gelände macht den starken Charakter dieser Räume aus. Die Leute erkennen sie wieder und nutzen sie auf vielfältige Weise. So werden Straße und Platz Teil des Viertels und erhalten Bedeutung.

Genau das erwarteten unsere Auftraggeber. Sie wünschten sich für den Stadtteil Navas einen neuen öffentlichen Freiraum, der auf dem Stadtplan Barcelonas deutlich zu erkennen ist. Wir untersuchten die Straßenführung des Viertels und fanden heraus, daß sich hier zwei Geometrien überlagern. Einst bestimmten die Calle Bofarull und der geschwungene Kanal des Rec Comptal den Stadtgrundriß, heute legt sich das streng orthogonale Cerdá-

urb: the emptiness between the buildings, the negative space to the architecture. We arranged the space so that it seems open and dynamic. Plain Euclidian shapes are disposed apparently arbitrarily on the square. In fact they pick up lines and directions we derived from the urban layout. Thus a continually new image of the city presents itself to the pedestrians from different standpoints. Being so firmly based in the terrain is what lends these spaces such a powerful character. People recognize them and use them in various ways. Thus the spaces become part of the neighbourhood and acquire meaning.

This is exactly what our clients expected. They wanted a new open public space for Navas, a part of the town, easy to find on the map of Barcelona. We examined the course of the streets in the area and discovered that two geometrical schemes overlap. Calle Bofarull and the winding Rec Comptal canal formerly determined the layout of the city; today the strictly orthogonal Cerdá grid is superimposed upon it. Almost all problems the quarter has in terms of urban planning can be traced back to this overlay: poor accessibility, streets without buildings, old structures, high density and marginality.

The Rec Comptal canal runs underground nowadays. Yet its irregular course can still be recognized in the lots along the Calle Bofarull. We have raised the canal to the leitmotiv of our design: we laid the new pavement on Calle Bofarull tangentially to the curves of the canal and planted vegetation along corresponding lines. Calle Bofarull thus becomes in a sense the riverbank promenade of Rec Comptal. The rows of trees follow the course of the old canal. Sometimes they divide and surround a clearing. The lines in

Calle Bofarull and Plaça d'Islandia, Sant Andreu, Barcelona
Client: City of Barcelona, District of Sant Andreu
Architects: Andreu Arriola, Carmen Fiol
Collaborators: Jane Opher, project architect; Agustí Obiol, statics;
Eugeni Frias, installations; Gaspar García, quantity surveyor
Size: 10 000 square metres
Planning period: 1993–1994
Construction period: 1994–April 1995
Costs: Pts 200 million

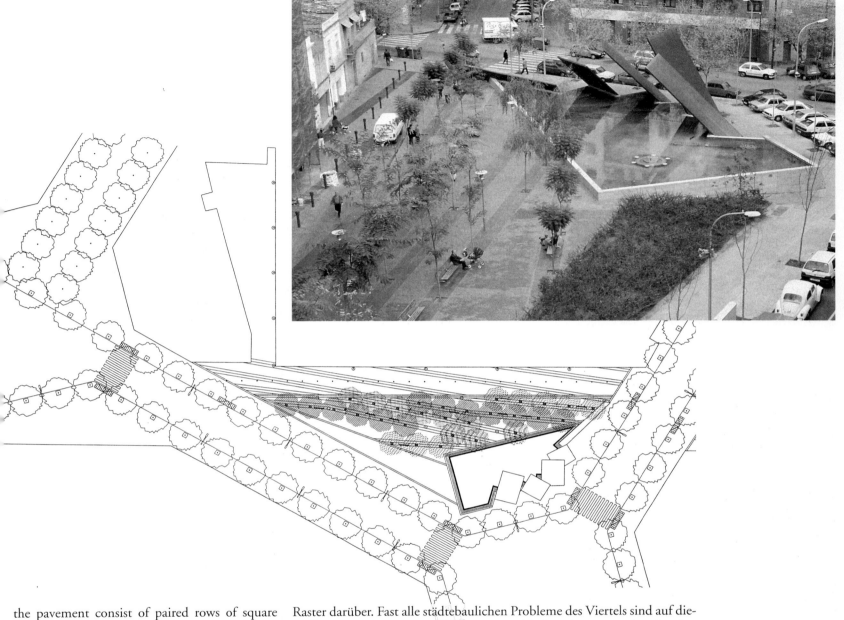

the pavement consist of paired rows of square slabs of Corten steel and concrete. Tree trunks rise from one row, lamp posts from the other. We planted locust trees, tipuana tipu and jacaranda acutifolia in rows, which bloom white, yellow and blue, respectively, in late spring and summer. We purposely chose a reddish terracotta pavement for Calle Bofarull to contrast with the familiar grey of the asphalt of Ensanche Cerdá. The dark red of the Corten steel and the light red

Raster darüber. Fast alle städtebaulichen Probleme des Viertels sind auf diese Überlagerung zurückzuführen: sein schlechter Zugang, seine Straßen ohne Bebauung, seine alte Bausubstanz, die hohe Dichte, die Marginalität.

Der Kanal Rec Comptal verläuft mittlerweile unterirdisch. An den Parzellen der Calle Bofarull aber kann man noch heute seinen unregelmäßigen Verlauf ablesen. Ihn haben wir zum Leitmotiv unseres Entwurfs erhoben: Tangential zu den Kurvenlinien des Kanals verlegten wir ein neues Pflaster auf der Calle Bofarull und pflanzten die Vegetation in entsprechenden Linien. Die Calle Bofarull wird so gewissermaßen zur Uferpromenade des Rec Comptal. Die Baumreihen folgen dem Verlauf des alten Kanals.

Wo die Calle Bofarull die Ecke eines Cerdá-Blocks abschneidet, gestalteten die Architekten einen Platz mit dem Charakter eines Gartens. Der Boden scheint aufzubrechen: Fünf große Platten aus Corten-Stahl schieben sich aus einem großen Wasserbecken. Ein künstlicher Geysir gibt dem Platz seinen Namen: Plaça d'Islandia.

Where Calle Bofarull cuts off a corner of the Cerdá grid, the architects created a square with a garden atmosphere. The ground seems to burst open: five large Corten steel plates emerge from a large pool. An artificial geyser gives the square its name: Plaça d'Islandia.

Auf der Plaça d'Islandia erinnern Wasserspiele an isländische Naturschauspiele. Um das Wasser des künstlichen Geysirs sprudeln und verdampfen zu lassen, installierten die Architekten einen zeitweilig rotierenden Wasserstrahl und Unterwasserpumpen. Fünf Wasserfälle – benannt nach ihren berühmten isländischen Vorbildern – entspringen an den Platten aus Corten-Stahl und verschwinden im Dampf.

The fountains in Plaça d'Islandia recall natural Icelandic water displays. To make the water bubble and vaporize around the artificial geyser, the architects installed an intermittently rotating water jet with underwater pumps. Five waterfalls, named after their famous Icelandic models, gush from the Corten steel plates and disappear in a cloud of vapour.

Manchmal teilen sie sich und umfassen eine Lichtung. Im Pflaster bestehen die vom Kanal abgeleiteten Linien aus einer Doppelreihe quadratischer Platten aus Corten-Stahl und Beton. Aus der einen erheben sich die Baumstämme, aus der anderen die Masten der Beleuchtung. Wir pflanzten Robinien, Tipuana tipu und Jacaranda acutifolia in Reihen, die im späten Frühling und im Sommer jeweils weiß, gelb und blau blühen. Für die Calle Bofarull wählten wir bewußt ein rötliches Terrakotta-Pflaster, das sich vom gewohnten Grau des Asphalts und der Betonplatten im Ensanche Cerdá absetzt. Das Dunkelrot des Corten-Stahls und die hellen Rottöne der Bodenplatten bestimmen den Straßenraum und erwecken den Eindruck von ursprünglichen Materialien aus der Zeit vor der Verstädterung.

Im Querschnitt ist die Calle Bofarull asymmetrisch aufgebaut. Auf der einen Seite haben wir eine Fahrspur angelegt. Eine Linie aus Pollern und Markierungen schützt die Eingänge zu Wohnhäusern und Geschäften vor dem Autoverkehr. Auf der anderen Seite schufen wir eine großzügige Allee für Fußgänger. Eine Linie aus Corten-Stahl und Beton und ein Belagswechsel trennt sie von der Fahrspur.

An der Kreuzung der Straßen Espronceda und Palencia taucht Wasser aus dem Untergrund auf. Sponsoren aus Island finanzierten einen künstlichen, 17 Meter hohen Geysir, den wir in ein 15 mal 33 Meter großes Becken mit mehreren Fontänen setzten. Wir haben dafür eine Freifläche an einer abgeschrägten Ecke des Cerdá-Rasters genutzt. Diesen neuen Platz nannten wir Plaça d'Islandia. Er bildet einen starken Gegensatz zum rationalen, auf den Verkehr abgestimmten Stadtgrundriß. Das Wasser, der Verzicht auf Autos, die Vegetation, ein neues Pflaster und das Stadtmobiliar verleihen dem Raum den Charakter eines Gartens. Er ist das Kernstück unserer Gestaltung, ein Entwurf im Maßstab der Stadt.

Um im Becken des künstlichen Geysirs das Wasser sprudeln und verdampfen zu lassen, kombinierten wir einen zeitweilig rotierenden Wasserstrahl mit Luftkompressoren und Unterwasserpumpen. Fünf große Corten-Stahlplatten schieben sich schräg in das Becken und zerschneiden die rechteckige Wasserfläche. Fünf Wasserfälle entspringen an den Platten und verschwinden in einer Wolke aus Dampf. Sie tragen die Namen von fünf isländischen Wasserfällen. Die Stahlplatten steigen von zwei auf acht Meter Höhe und wirken wie Erdschollen, die sich aus dem Boden schieben. Wer zwischen ihnen hindurchgeht, fühlt sich der Erde, dem Wasser und dem Himmel verbunden.

tones of the pavement slabs define the street space and give the impression of natural materials from the days before urbanization.

In cross-section Calle Bofarull is built up asymmetrically. We ran a wide car lane along one side. A line of bollards and traffic signals shields the entrances to residential buildings and shops from car traffic. Along the opposite side, we made a generous sidewalk. A line of Corten steel and concrete and a change in pavement distinguish it from the car lane.

At the intersection of Espronceda and Palencia Streets is a subterranean spring. Icelandic sponsors funded an artificial 17-metre geyser, which we enclosed in a 15-by-33-metre pool with several fountains. We made use of a free space on a cut-off corner of the Cerdá grid for it. We called this new square Plaça d'Islandia (Iceland Square). It forms a powerful contrast to the urban layout that is determined by traffic. The water, the absence of cars, the vegetation, new pavement and urban furniture invest the place with the atmosphere of a garden. It is the core of our design, planned on the scale of the city.

To make the water bubble and vaporize in the artificial geyser pool, we combined an intermittently rotating water jet with air compressors and underwater pumps. Five large Corten steel plates edge into the pool at an angle, cutting into the rectangular surface of the water. Five waterfalls gushing from the plates disappear in a cloud of vapour. They bear the names of five Icelandic waterfalls. The steel plates rise from two to eight metres in height, looking like chunks of earth bursting out of the ground. Anyone running around between them feels in touch with the earth, the water and the sky.

Reykjavík: Rathaus am Seeufer

A lakeside city hall for Reykjavík

The project for Reykjavík City hall was won in a competition in 1987. The site was an open lot in the north-western corner of Tjörnin, a man-made lake in the city centre of Reykjavík. A landscape plan for the northern end of the lake was also part of the competition. To the north of the site is the parliament, cathedral and commercial centre of the city. To the south, across the lake, are long views to the mountains on the far side of the bay.

The buildings surrounding the site are comprised of a chaotic mix of scales, styles, materials and colours. This lack of a strong architectural identity encouraged a design concept which drew its sources not only from the immediate area but from the wider context of Icelandic nature and landscape with its magical light, mass, form and perceptual trickery. The challenge was to balance the contrasting permanence of the city and the delicate ecology of the lake by means of an understanding and extrapolation of their essential qualities rather than by imposing a new order.

Reflecting the dual nature of the location, the winning design split the city hall into two parts, a city council building and an office building. To the north the City Council Building is massive and orthogonal, respecting the urban scale and order of the existing city fabric.

To the south the Office Building has a lighter structure, and is open to the lake and veiled in a filigree dance of shadows. This association with existing conditions is reversed on the city side by folding the lake into the city in the form of a pool, above which the city council chamber window hovers like a giant lantern. The Office Building, clad with thick, lava-encrusted panels, forms the southern boundary to this pool. A

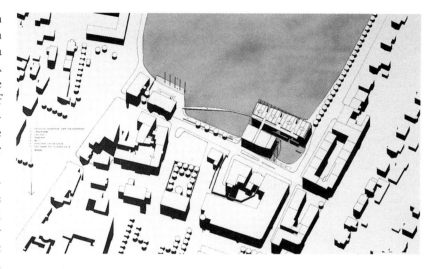

Das neue Rathaus der Stadt Reykjavík und seine Außenanlagen beziehen sich auf ein freies Gelände am nordwestlichen Ufer des Tjörnin, einem künstlich angelegten See im Zentrum der Stadt. Zu diesem Projekt gehörte auch ein Landschaftsplan für die Nordseite des Sees. In unmittelbarer Nachbarschaft des neuen Rathauses befinden sich das Parlament, die Kathedrale, das Handelszentrum Reykjavíks und eine chaotische Bebauung aus verschiedenen Stilen, Baumaterialien, Farben und Bauhöhen. Im Süden, jenseits des Sees, erstreckt sich das weite Panorama der Berge.

Gerade wegen des Mangels an klarer architektonischer Identität schlugen wir für den Rathausneubau ein Planungskonzept vor, das sich nicht nur nach der unmittelbaren Nachbarschaft richtete, sondern darüber hinaus die gesamte isländische Natur und Landschaft mit ihrem magischen Licht und den daraus resultierenden optischen Eindrücken einbezog. Die sich widersprechenden Aspekte der modernen Stadt und des empfindlichen ökologischen Gleichgewichts des Sees wollten wir zu einer Harmonie verschmelzen lassen – nicht durch das Überstülpen einer neuen Ordnung, sondern indem wir die Qualitäten dieser Gegensätze gestalterisch hervorhoben.

Das neue Rathaus spiegelt die Dualität seiner

Steve Christer

Das neue Rathaus von Reykjavík und seine Außenanlagen beziehen sich auf den Tjörnin, den großen See im Zentrum der Stadt.
The landscaping at the new city hall of Reykjavík relates to Lake Tjörnin, a man-made body of water in the city's heart.

Das neue Rathaus von Reykjavík öffnet sich nach Süden (im Plan oben) zum künstlich angelegten Tjörnin-See. Im Norden nimmt ein zweiter, strengerer Baukörper die Geometrie der angrenzenden Gebäude auf. Ein öffentlicher Weg im Erdgeschoß führt zwischen beiden Gebäudeteilen hindurch auf eine Brücke im Osten, die zum eschenbestandenen Ufer überleitet.

The new city hall in Reykjavík opens up to an artificial lake to the south, its geometry repeated by a second, more austere building to the north. A public ground-floor path leads between and through the buildings to a bridge in the east, from where it continues to a bank planted with ash trees.

Materialdetails am neuen Rathaus von Reykjavík: Tafeln mit Erläuterungen zur Vogelwelt, die Ufermauer mit auskragenden Sitzbänken und Wasserspeiern, die wasserberieselte Mooswand aus Lavagestein.

Details of the new city hall in Reykjavík: information panels on bird life, the waterfront quay with its benches and waterspouts, and a wall of volcanic rock that features water, moss and ice.

Als Kontrast zum Beton, Glas und Aluminium des Rathauses verwendeten die Architekten im Außenraum Basalt für die Mauern sowie Granit und Beton für die Pflasterwege, Rampen und Treppen.

As a contrast to the concrete, glass and aluminium of the city hall, the architects of Studio Granda used basalt for the outside walls and granite and concrete for pathways, ramps and steps.

trough, filled with ground water from a nearby well, occupies the adjacent roof.

The water spills over the edge to trickle down the black lava in sparkling droplets, creating ideal conditions for moss growth. The moss wall is not an attempt to make nature, it is the creation of a condition which nature may inhabit. Likewise the pool provides a new home for trout, salmon and a pair of mallards.

In its former function as a car park, the site served the purpose of a short-cut for pedestrians. The ground floor of the City Hall is organised around the memory of these walking routes and as a consequence has no formal entrance. The intention is for it to be used again as a short cut by citizens and visitors and to get them involved in activities in the public halls.

A café encourages people to linger and enjoy the view. During the long winter months the lake-side steps of the City Hall café are a popular rendezvous for skaters seeking warm refreshments. On the east side of the building the routes are extended in the form of a bridge leading to Iðnó small wooden theatre.

The City Hall is constructed out of concrete, glass and aluminium, all precision-manufactured materials.

However, the design is conceived in such a way that it will be perceived not only as a combination of these innate elements but as a living organism enlivened by the play of light, shadow and parallax effects. By contrast the surrounding landscape works are more earth-bound and straightforward. The main built elements are low, hewn basalt walls which demarcate changes of level and provide shelter. The rough, hand-worked character of the walls creates the impres-

Umgebung durch seine Aufteilung in zwei Bereiche wider. Im Norden steht das massive und orthogonale Regierungsgebäude. Es paßt sich den existierenden Bauten der Umgebung an. Nach Süden öffnet sich der zweite Teil des Gebäudes, die Verwaltung, mit einer leichteren Struktur zum See, wobei das Licht zarte Schatten auf der Fassade tanzen läßt. Dieser Teil des Gebäudes scheint im See zu stehen – in Wirklichkeit ist ein Becken gebaut worden, das die Wasserfläche unter dem Bauwerk durchführt. Das Fenster des Sitzungssaals schwebt wie eine riesige Laterne über diesem glatten Spiegel. Die Mauern des Verwaltungsgebäudes sind zum Teich hin mit Lavagestein

Der südliche Gebäudeteil des neuen Rathauses von Reykjavík scheint auf Stützen im Tjörnin-See zu stehen. In Wirklichkeit ist ein Becken gebaut worden, das die Wasserfläche unter dem Bauwerk hindurchführt. Vom Café im Erdgeschoß überblicken die Besucher den See. Während der Wintermonate verwandeln sich seine Treppen zum Treffpunkt für Schlittschuhläufer.

The southern section of the new city hall in Reykjavík seems to stand on pillars in the lake, but was actually erected above a basin into which water was then let. The steps leading down to the lake from the ground-storey café, which provides pleasant views of the water, are popular with ice-skaters during the winter.

sion that were the first objects installed by man in the area. This manipulation of time aids their integration into the city fabric and helps create a coherent context with the City Hall. Observant visitors may also notice that the precast concrete copings echo the form of the roof of City Hall.

Paving, ramps and steps in a mixture of granite and concrete slabs, paviors and basaltic stones are conceived as a horizontal extension of the walls. Patterns are minimised to identify usage and in this way embellish the ground planes. At the lake edge, large hewn basalt stones provide a strong visual border that contrasts with the rhythmic movement of waves.

In the same way that City Hall attempts to relate the city to the lake, so too the landscaping is concerned with the interface between man and the rich fauna of Tjörnin. A series of precast concrete and cantilevered steel benches are strategically located for people to enjoy their free time in the special environment of the lake. In front of Iðnó, a bench is further enhanced by information plates displaying the species of birds and their living habits, and young ducklings are able to access the walkways by means of ramps set at regular intervals. The waterfowl which remain in Iceland during the winter are provided an improved habitat as a result of the geothermal hot water system, which maintains snow and ice-free pavements in winter. The residue heat from this system is discharged into the lake through three steel gargoyles to keep the north-eastern corner of the pond free of ice.

Plantings are used to reinforce the main ideas of the project and to soften the boundary between man-made and natural elements. In the

verkleidet. Darüber läuft Wasser, das aus einem nahegelegenen Brunnen stammt – der ideale Nährboden für Moosbewuchs. Diese Mooswand soll nicht versuchen, Natur zu erschaffen, sondern vielmehr eine Umwelt bieten, die von der Natur genutzt wird. Ebenso dient das Becken unter dem Gebäude Forellen, Lachsen und einem Wildentenpärchen als Lebensraum.

Bevor das Rathaus erbaut wurde, diente das Gelände als Parkplatz und wurde von den Fußgängern als Abkürzung durch die Stadt benutzt. Das Erdgeschoß des Rathauses trägt dieser Funktion Rechnung: Statt eines großartigen Eingangs legten wir einen Weg durch das Rathaus an die gleiche Abkürzung wie seit jeher. So werden die Bewohner und Besucher der Stadt ganz nebenbei mit den Aktivitäten in den »öffentlichen Hallen« vertraut gemacht. Ein Café soll dazu ermuntern, zu verweilen und den Anblick zu genießen. Während der Wintermonate verwandeln sich die Treppen vom Café zum See hinab zum beliebten Treffpunkt für Schlittschuhläufer, die eine Stärkung zu sich nehmen wollen. Im Osten wird der Weg über eine Brücke verlängert, die über das gekräuselte Wasser zum »Iðnó« führt, einem kleinen Theatergebäude aus Holz.

Das Rathaus besteht aus Beton, Glas und Aluminium. Der Betrachter nimmt jedoch nicht nur eine Kombination dieser drei Baustoffe wahr, sondern einen Körper, dem das Spiel von Licht und Schatten Leben einhaucht. Im Gegensatz dazu erscheinen die Außenanlagen erdgebunden. Niedrige, behauene Basaltmauern bestimmen die Gestaltung und betonen zum einen den Wechsel von einer Ebene zur nächsten, zum anderen bieten sie Schutz. Diese Mauern vermitteln den Eindruck, sie seien die ersten Zeugen menschlichen Wirkens in dieser Gegend – ein Spiel mit der Geschichte, das die Integration in das Stadtbild erleichtert und einen Bezug zum Rathaus herstellt. Der aufmerksame Betrachter wird feststellen, daß die vorgegossenen Mauerkronen aus Beton die Form des Rathausdaches wiederholen.

Pflasterwege, Rampen und Treppen bestehen aus Granit und Betonplatten, Gehwegpflaster und Basaltsteine und bilden horizontale Erweiterungen der Mauern. Muster ergeben sich lediglich durch den Wechsel des Materials, der wiederum durch die Nutzung bestimmt ist. Am Seeufer werden große, behauene Basaltsteine zur eindrucksvollen optischen Grenze, die im Kontrast zu den rhythmischen Wellenbewegungen steht.

So wie das Rathaus eine Verbindung von der Stadt zum See schafft, bilden die Außenanlagen eine Schnittstelle zwischen den Menschen und der reichhaltigen Fauna des Tjörnin. Eine Reihe von vorgefertigten Betonbän-

Reykjavík City Hall
Client: City of Reykjavík
Design: Steve Christer, Margrét
Harðardóttir (Studio Granda), architects
Competition: 1987
Construction: 1988–1992
Size of public areas: 1 300 square metres

ken und freitragenden Stahlbänken stellten wir so auf, daß man von dort aus die außergewöhnliche Umgebung des Sees betrachten kann. Vor dem »Iðnó« wurden an einer Bank Informationstafeln über die hier lebenden Vogelarten und ihre Lebensgewohnheiten angebracht. Damit sich Menschen und Vögel »näherkommen«, gibt es für die Entenküken in regelmäßigen Abständen kleine Rampen zu den Gehwegen. Das geothermale Heißwassersystem, das die Wege im Winter schnee- und eisfrei hält, erleichtert den Wasservögeln das Überwintern. Das warme Restwasser dieses Systems wird über drei stählerne Wasserspeier in den See geleitet, um den Nordostteil eisfrei zu halten.

Die Bepflanzung unterstützt den Übergang von den künstlichen zu den natürlichen Bereichen. Als Straßenbäume wählten wir Eschen, die im Sommer weiche Alleen mit vollem Laub und im Winter malerische Silhouetten bilden. Sträucher beleben die Fußwege – farblich abgestimmt zu dem kühlen Grau der Gebäude und dem warmen Braun des Basalts. In geschützten Bereichen wurden empfindlichere Pflanzen gepflanzt, und über die langen Basaltmauern ließen wir Efeu ranken.

streets ash has been planted formally to create soft avenues with lush leaves in summer and graphic silhouettes in winter. Flowering shrubs enliven and provide shelter to paths, with a range of blossoms chosen to complement the cool grey of the building and the warm brown basalt. In sheltered areas, smaller, more delicate growth has been introduced and ivy inhabits the long, ruinous basalt walls.

A city hall ist symbolically the heart of a metropolis. This project aims to interpret and reinforce the conditions which allow the city of Reykjavík to exist to enable the building to credibly fulfil that role. Consequently, the individual elements of the project are less important than the calm and seemingly inevitable way in which they fit together.

Da es dem Nordufer des Tjörnin-Sees in Reykjavík an klarer architektonischer Identität fehlte, entwarfen die Architekten von »Studio Granda« ein Rathaus, das als Landmarke über dem See zu schweben scheint. Die Gestaltung von Gebäude und Außenanlagen bezieht die isländische Natur und Landschaft mit ihrem magischen Licht ein.

Since the northern bank of Tjörnin Lake in Reykjavík was clearly lacking in architectural identity, the Studio Granda planners wanted to create a landmark, and the result is a city hall that seems to hover above the lake. The building and the outdoor facilities incorporate elements of Icelandic nature, with the magical light of Iceland landscapes.

Docklands, London: Am Anfang war der Platz

Docklands, London: In the beginning there was a space

The London Docklands have been the focus for regeneration in London since the economic boom of the early eighties. Then the creation of an "Enterprise Zone" on the Isle of Dogs was aimed at attracting new businesses and encouraging City firms to re-locate eastwards away from their traditional London heartlands into a new dynamic environment. Twenty years on there is another concerted move to push further eastwards – to open up the miles of the Royal Docklands that spread out along the Thames. EDAW was commissioned by the London Development Agency to design a new square and propose a revised development framework for the Royals that embraced the existing development proposals as well as reinforcing the waterfronts and the open space network between them.

The Royal Docks are at once a challenging and inspirational environment; one cannot fail to be moved by the sheer scale of the man-made structures, huge expanses of water and hard-standings, towering dock cranes and abandoned warehouses. However, what really strikes you is the impact of the skyscape, the broad horizons and often-penetrating wind and the constant distraction and animation of low-flying aircraft landing at the adjacent city airport

Royal Victoria Square is at the hub of the new open space network of the Royal Docks. The Square fronts Victoria Dock and the recently opened London Exhibition Centre. It also lies on a natural pedestrian route from the recently built Silvertown "urban village" south of the dock to the Docklands Light Railway to the north.

Conceived as a new London space to rival the attraction and scale of famous landmarks such as Trafalgar Square and Leicester Square, it has tak-

Seit dem Wirtschaftsboom Anfang der 80er Jahre sind die London Docklands Brennpunkt der Stadterneuerung in London. Damals wurde auf der Isle of Dogs eine »Wirtschaftszone« mit dem Ziel gegründet, neue Unternehmen anzuziehen und Firmen aus der City weiter nach Osten in die neue Umgebung zu locken. Nun, zwanzig Jahre danach, gibt es eine neue Bewegung noch weiter nach Osten: Man will die meilenlangen Royal Docklands am Themseufer erschließen. Das Büro EDAW erhielt von der London Development Agency den Auftrag, einen neuen Stadtplatz zu entwerfen und ein revidiertes Rahmenwerk für die Entwicklung der »Royals« zu erstellen. Unter Berücksichtigung bestehender Ent-

David Allen

Den Royal Victoria Square mussten die Landschaftsarchitekten als Platz gestalten, dem die angrenzende Bebauung noch fehlt.

The Royal Victoria Square had to be designed without knowing which buildings would one day surround it.

Eckpfeiler des Gestaltungskonzeptes waren die Zeugen der industriellen Vergangenheit: ein historischer Speicher und die 20 Meter hohen Kräne, die den Blick über die Wasserfläche des Victoria-Docks am südlichen Platzrand rahmen.

Witnesses of the industrial past were taken as the cornerstones of the design concept. These consist of a historic warehouse and 20-meter-high dockyard cranes that frame views of the expanse of water at Victoria Docks.

Präzise ausgearbeitete Ränder aus Granit, Cortenstahl und großen Mauerkronen fassen den zentralen Rasen. Im Flugdach dahinter eingelassen sind Namen großer Schiffe, die ehemals den Hafen frequentierten (rechts).

The central lawn is held by a series of highly-detailed edges of granite, Corten steel and large copings. Names of the past great ships that used the dock are cut into a brise soleil extending from the top of the canopy (right).

wicklungsplanungen sollen die Bereiche am Wasser sowie das verbindende Netz öffentlicher Räume aufgewertet werden.

Die Royal Docks sind Herausforderung und Inspiration gleichermaßen. Jeder ist von der schieren Größe der Bauwerke, den riesigen Wasserflächen und Einbauten, den turmhohen Kränen in den Hafenbecken und den verlassenen Speichergebäuden beeindruckt. Aber am meisten imponiert der Himmel: der weite Horizont, der Wind und die ständige Ablenkung durch Flugzeuge im Landeanflug auf den benachbarten City-Flughafen. Der Royal Victoria Square ist der Angelpunkt des neuen Netzes von öffentlichen Räumen in den Royal Docks. Der Platz grenzt an das Victoria Dock, an das vor kurzem eröffnete London Exhibition Centre und an eine Fußwegverbindung zwischen dem kürzlich erbauten »städtischen Quartier« Silverton, südlich vom Dock und der nördlich gelegenen, die Docklands erschließenden Bahnlinie.

Hier sollte ein neuer Platz in London entstehen, der in Anziehungskraft und Größe Wahrzeichen wie Trafalgar Square und Leicester Square Paroli bieten kann. Vom ersten Konzept bis hin zur Vollendung dauerte es fünf Jahre. Anders als bei den meisten Stadtplätzen gab es hier kaum Einschränkungen durch bestehende Bauwerke. Die Planer konnten die Ausdehnung des Platzes definieren und seine Form frei erfinden. Der südliche Rand des Platzes grenzt an die ausgedehnte Wasserfläche des Victoria-Docks. Die einzigen Originalbauwerke auf dem Gelände – ein historischer Speicher und mehrere 20 Meter hohe Kräne – stellen Bezüge zur Geschichte und zur Industrie her. Sie wurden schließlich zu den visuellen Eckpfeilern für das Gestaltungskonzept.

Anfangs war es eine Herausforderung, die Ausmaße des Raumes zu erfassen und sich vor Augen zu halten, wie neue Baumaßnahmen zur Gestalt und zum baulichen Rahmen des Platzes beitragen würden. Diese sind nun projektiert und sollen einen lebendigen Nutzungsmix schaffen: ein Hotel für Erholungsuchende und eines für Geschäftsleute, Büros, ein Nachtlokal, Läden und Wohnungen.

en five years from conceptual design to completion. Unlike most other urban squares, the site was largely unconstrained by existing buildings, giving the designers the opportunity to define the extent of the square and manipulate the forms of its enclosure.

The southern edge of the square faces across the wide water of the Victoria Dock. The only original built references on the site are a historic warehouse and several 20-meter-high dockyard cranes providing the square's historic and industrial context and ultimately the visual keys that unlocked the design concept.

One of the challenges at the early stages was to understand the scale of the space and to envisage the contribution that future developments would make to the setting and containment of the space. These projects are now being drawn up to create an active mix of uses around the Square, including a boutique hotel, business hotel, offices, night club, shops and apartments.

The industrial honesty of the existing warehouse and the loading cranes that framed views across the expanse of water became central in the

initial design studies. The importance of these elements was subsequently confirmed by historical research, which revealed that the central part of the square was originally a "finger" dock allowing the sailing ships and barges of the 18th and 19th century to unload their cargo of tobacco and oranges directly into the warehouse.

The emerging composition identified the space between the warehouse and the cranes as the "main" square or "void" around which the other spaces could function as anterooms, thresholds and settings. In the final design, this centrepiece became a pure plane of grass inclined towards the water and held by a series of highly-detailed edges of granite, Corten steel and large copings that turn into the space from the principle dock edge, indicating the space's original function as a finger dock.

At the southern end of the main square is a steel deck that hovers over the dark water of the main dock, allowing people to closely connect with this often forbidding element. Further framing the main square's vertical edges are two bold canopies that run down each side, completing the enclosure of the central void like huge black concrete fins of a scale that reflects but does not compete with the loading cranes. Simple seating positioned under the canopy provides the opportunity to sit and enjoy the expanse across and through the space.

Across the northern side of the main square, a ceremonial route was devised which focuses on the monumental steps and entrance of the Exhibition Centre and provides a number of celebratory experiences for visitors entering the Square. Alongside, two lines of 36 computer-controlled fountain jets rise and fall in a wave motion. Optic fibre lighting is used to control groups of jets rising from eccentric stainless steel grills set into ground, creating movement, light and sound, heightening the senses and creating a fun play area.

Finally, before arriving at the base of the Exhibition Centre steps, visitors walk through a field of random kinetic wands which stitch together the joining of spaces and move gently in

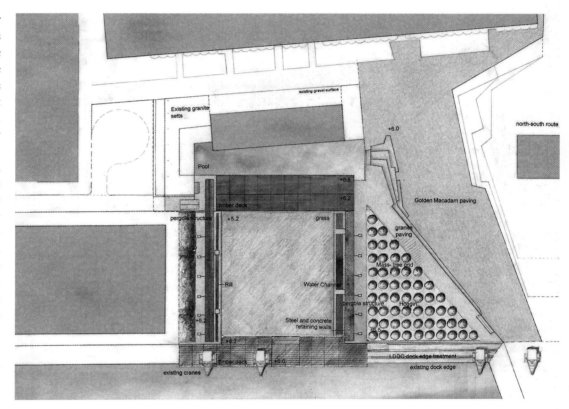

Der industrielle Charakter des Speicherhauses und die Ladekräne, die den Blick über die weite Wasserfläche rahmen, spielten in den Vorentwurfsskizzen eine zentrale Rolle. Wie wichtig diese Elemente waren, bestätigte schließlich ein Blick in die Geschichte: Der zentrale Teil des Platzes war ursprünglich ein fingerförmiges, eigens angelegtes Hafenbecken, das den Segelschiffen und Barkassen im 18. und 19. Jahrhundert das Entladen von Tabak und Orangen direkt in den Speicher ermöglichte.

Im entstehenden Entwurf wurde der Raum zwischen dem Speicher und den Kränen zum Hauptplatz oder »Leerraum«. Um ihn herum angelegte öffentliche Räume sollten als Vorzimmer, Schwelle und Hintergrund fungieren. Im endgültigen Entwurf wurde diese zentrale Fläche zu einer zum Wasser geneigten Grasfläche, gefasst von präzise ausgearbeiteten Rändern

Die zentrale Rasenfläche erinnert an ein Hafenbecken, das den Segelschiffen und Barkassen direkten Zugang zum Speicher ermöglichte. Im Westen begrenzt ein dreieckiger Obstbaumhain den Platz.

The central area of lawn, which is reminiscent of the finger dock that enabled sailing ships and barges to unload their cargo into the warehouse, is flanked to the west by a triangular orchard space.

Zwei Reihen von Fontänen, jede einzelne von Leuchtfasern beleuchtet, erheben sich an der Nordseite des Platzes aus Gittern aus rostfreiem Stahl. Die Fontänen bewegen sich wellenförmig auf und ab.

Two lines of fountain jets emerge from stainless steel grills let into the paving at the northern end of the square, whereby fibre optics light the cores of water as they rise and fall in a wave-like motion.

aus Granit, Cortenstahl und großen Mauerkronen, die vom Rand des Victoria-Docks in den Platz greifen und somit seine historische Funktion als Hafenbecken andeuten.

Am südlichen Ende des Hauptplatzes befindet sich ein Deck aus Stahl über dem dunklen Wasser des Beckens, das den Menschen engen Kontakt zu diesem oft beängstigenden Element ermöglicht. Zwei kühne Flugdächer bilden zudem senkrechte Ränder des Hauptplatzes und rahmen zusätzlich den zentralen Raum. Diese riesigen flossenförmigen Strukturen aus schwarzem Beton spielen mit ihrer Größe auf die Hafenkräne an, sollen aber nicht mit ihnen wetteifern. Auf einfachen Sitzgelegenheiten unter den Flugdächern kann man sich niederlassen und die Weite des Raumes genießen.

Entlang der Nordseite des Hauptplatzes führt ein festlich anmutender Weg zur monumentalen Treppe und zum Eingang des Exhibition Centre. Zwei Reihen von 36 computergesteuerten Fontänen bewegen sich entlang des Weges wellenförmig auf und ab. Lichtfaserkabel steuern Gruppen von Fontänen, die sich aus ausgefallenen Gittern aus rostfreiem Stahl auf Bodenniveau erheben.

Schließlich gehen Besucher auf dem Weg zu den Stufen zum Exhibition Center durch ein Feld von wie zufällig verstreuten kinetischen Ruten. Sie verbinden die Räume miteinander und schaukeln sanft im Wind – eine subtile Erinnerung an die sich stets ändernde Umwelt. Die Glasfaser-Ruten stehen auf einem robusten Holzsockel, der um 15 Grad verkantet ist, und erinnern an die vielen Schiffsmasten im Hafenbecken. Die Bündel roter Leuchtdioden am Ende der Masten schwanken hin und her wie Positionslichter von Schiffen.

the wind – a subtle reminder of the ever-changing environment. The wands are made of glass fibre. Rising out of a robust wooden base and canted over at 15 degrees, they are reminiscent of ships masts crowded in the dock. The lighting unit at the mast top is a red cluster LED that sway like ship navigation lights.

Between the main square and the Exhibition Centre, a triangular orchard space allows through movement and free desire lines where the pedestrian routes meet. This space was originally conceived as containing a possible pavilion building to counter the vastness of the Exhibition Centre, but no suitable use was forthcoming. The orchard successfully creates the same sense of mass and substance of a building whilst having the advantage of softening views. The softer colours and types of materials in this area contrast with the main square and aim to invoke the simplicity of a gravel drive leading up to a stately home. The trees of the orchard are boxed-up, forming a roof to the space and giving it a special character within the overall square.

Across Royal Victoria Square, lighting has been employed to ensure that the space is as in-

Royal Victoria Square, Royal Docklands, London
Lead design consultant: EDAW – David Allen, Warren Osborne
Client: London Development Agency
Engineers: Aspen Burrow Crocker
Architect: Patel Taylor
Costs: GBP 3.2 Million
Size: 16,000 square metres
Construction: 2000

teresting at night as it is during the day. In addition to standard column lights along the dock edge, a number of lighting features reinforce the design concepts. Around the edge of the central lawn, a fibre optic is embedded in the lip of the coping to downlight the inclining walls and reinforce the edge of the finger dock. Uplighters under the canopy emphasise its height and fibre optics within each fountain jet light the cores of water as they rise and fall. Ground-level lighting washes across the ceremonial route, and the kinetic wands contain glowing red diodes which contrast and move against the black skies.

Further references to the industrial past have also been subtly included to promote a sense of discovery in the visitor. Names of the past great ships that used the dock are cut into a brise soleil extending from the top of the canopy. The letter notations E & F, which identified the two piers of the past finger dock, are moulded into the top of the canopy fins and cut into the new steel abutments along the ceremonial route.

Royal Victoria Square was formally opened by the London mayor in December 2000 and has seen a growing number of visitors as the Exhibition Centre is now fully operational. In the future, as the remaining development sites come forward, the Square will function as an extended dining area, a setting for residents, an external exhibition space, a through space, a park and a gathering space.

Ein dreieckiger Obstbaumhain zwischen dem Platz und dem Exhibition Centre erlaubt freies Durchgehen und somit das Entstehen von Trampelpfaden. Der Hain erweckt ähnlich einem Gebäude das Gefühl von Masse und Substanz, hat aber den Vorteil, dass Sichtbeziehungen möglich sind. Die gedämpften Farben und Materialien in diesem Bereich stehen im Kontrast zum Hauptplatz. Die Obstbäume sind spalierartig hochgezogen. So entsteht ein Dach und dieser Raum erhält innerhalb des Platzes seinen eigenen Charakter.

Die Beleuchtung soll den Royal Victoria Square nachts ebenso interessant erscheinen lassen, wie er tagsüber ist. Zusätzlich zu den üblichen Lichtmasten am Hafenbecken unterstreichen Lichtanlagen die Absichten des Entwurfs. Um den zentralen Rasenplatz wurde ein Leuchtfaserkabel in den Überstand der Mauerkrone eingelassen, um die schräg abfallende Mauer von oben zu beleuchten und den Rand des historischen Hafenbeckens zu betonen. Nach oben gerichtete Strahler unter den Flugdächern betonen ihre Höhe und ihren optischen Schwebezustand. Lichtquellen aus Leuchtfasern in jedem Wasserstrahl beleuchten die auf- und absteigenden Wasserspiele. Eine Beleuchtung auf Bodenebene scheint über den Weg zu wischen und die kinetischen Ruten enthalten rote Leuchtdioden, die gegen den schwarzen Himmel Kontrast und Bewegung vermitteln.

Weitere Anspielungen an die industrielle Vergangenheit des Ortes wurden subtil eingebracht. Namen ehemals großer Schiffe, die diesen Hafen anliefen, sind in eine Sonnenblende eingelassen, die sich vom Dach des Flugdaches aus erstreckt. Die Buchstaben E & F, die die beiden Anlegestellen des einstigen Docks bezeichneten, wurden in die Spitze der Flossen an der Überdachung eingegossen und in Stahlstreben entlang des Weges eingraviert.

Im Dezember 2000 wurde der Royal Victoria Square feierlich durch den Bürgermeister von London eröffnet. Seit das Exhibition Centre den vollen Betrieb aufgenommen hat, ist auch die Besucherzahl des Platzes gestiegen. Wenn die geplanten Projekte verwirklicht werden, wird sich der Platz mit Straßencafés füllen, als Wohnumwelt für die Anwohner dienen, als Freiluft-Ausstellungsgelände, als Durchgang, Park und Treffpunkt.

Die Flugdächer aus schwarzem Beton, senkrechte Ränder des zentralen Platzes, werden von unten angestrahlt. Ihre Größe und ihr Maßstab orientierten sich an den Hafenkränen.

The two black concrete canopies that frame the main square's vertical edges are lit from below. Their scale reflects but does not compete with that of the cranes.

Irland: Neue Stadträume mit maßgeschneiderter Ausstattung

Ireland: New urban spaces and tailored fittings

Feargus McGarvey

Obwohl die irische Landschaftsarchitektur kaum Tradition in der Gestaltung ihrer öffentlichen Räume hat, gibt es interessante Beispiele. Despite little tradition in open space design, Irish landscape architecture can boast a number of striking urban spaces.

Bevor in Irland der derzeitige Wirtschaftsboom einsetzte, gab es nur wenige neue Projekte im städtischen Freiraum, über die zu schreiben sich lohnte. Charakteristisch für die Landschaftsarchitektur im Irland des späten 20. Jahrhunderts sind zurückhaltende, bescheidene Projekte, oft im städtebaulichen Maßstab. Die wichtigsten Plätze in unseren Städten sind einfache Straßenkreuzungen, die einen Platz bilden – oft werden sie als »diamonds« (Rauten) bezeichnet. Die meisten entstanden im frühen 17. Jahrhundert. Ihre Form hat sich über die Jahrhunderte hinweg kaum verändert, nur oberflächliche Markierungen, Beläge und der übliche Kram, der mit ihrer Funktion als Verkehrsknotenpunkt oder Marktplatz zusammenhängt, kamen hinzu.

Obwohl wir nun eine unabhängige, multikulturelle Nation mit Erfolg und Geld sind, gibt es in unserer Volkskultur keine Vorbilder für die Gestaltung unserer öffentlichen Räume. Genauso wenig haben wir Planer politischen Widerhall – zumindest in der Republik Irland. Wie sollen wir unsere Orte gestalten und wie ausstatten, um unserer Kultur Ausdruck zu verleihen? Wie soll ohne eine bestimmte Bildersprache ein ortsgebundener Stil entstehen? Die vier neuen Plätze, die in diesem Artikel beschrieben werden, stehen gleichermaßen für eine neue Haltung gegenüber städtischen Räumen und für unseren neuen Reichtum. Sie wurden alle von öffentlichen Organisationen beauftragt und unterstreichen ihre Eigenart mit Hilfe eigens gestalteter Ausstattung.

Ein Fähranleger. 1991 gab die Schifffahrtsbehörde einen neuen Fähranleger in Dun Laoghaire im südlichen County Dublin in Auftrag. Eine neue Superfähre sollte von dort über die Irische See nach Holyhead übersetzen. Ein neuer Stadtplatz sollte zum Ein- und Ausgang für die zu Fuß eintreffenden Passagiere der Fähre und zum öffentlichen Raum für die Einwohner werden. Das Herzstück des Entwurfs ist eine Fußgängerachse, die von der Hauptstraße des Ortes über den Eingang des Anlegers hin zum Platz führt. Sie wird durch eine Reihe von Beleuchtungskörpern flankiert und betont. Sie lenken auch die Bewegungsabläufe über den Platz hinweg in geeignete Bahnen. Dies wird durch eine 35 Meter lange geschwungene Bank mit Durchbrüchen zur Ostseite hin gefördert. Der Platz erhält seine Form durch das Terminal im Westen, die nördlichen und die östli-

Until the current economic boom kicked in, there were few new urban projects to write about. Landscape architecture in late 20th-century Ireland is characterised by low key, modest and intelligent interventions, often at a planning scale. The key spaces in our towns evolved simply from the junctions of roads forming a square – frequently referred to as 'diamonds'. These 'diamonds' are most associated with plantation settlements dating from the early 17th century. Their form has changed little over the centuries, other than superficial delineation and surfacing and general clutter associated with their evolving function as traffic junctions or markets.

Although we now have an independent, multi-cultural nation, with economic success and money to spend, we also have no ethnic design precedent for our public spaces, and neither do we have a political drum to beat – at least in the republic. How should we make our places and how should we furnish them to express ourselves, and how should we achieve a sense of place without icons? The four new spaces in this article are expressive of a new consciousness of our city spaces, and of our new wealth. They are all commissioned by public organisations, and they all use specially designed furniture to enhance their identity.

A ferry terminal. In 1991, the Department of the Marine commissioned a new ferry terminal at Dun Laoghaire, in South County Dublin in order to facilitate a new superferry on the Irish Sea crossing from Holyhead. A plaza was needed for the arrival and departure of foot passengers, and to be used as a new civic space for the citizens of the locality. The plan hangs on a spine of circulation leading from the main street to the terminal entrance onto the space. This is emphasised by a flanking line of lights, which also filters movement across the space, movement which is further filtered by a 35-metre-long serpentine seat with breaks towards the eastern side. The space is formed by the terminal building on the west, with the north and east sides closed by a 1.5 metre wall. This creates a sheltered microclimate away from the sea breeze, and draws people to its edge to watch activities in the harbour, and the arrival and departure of the ferry.

On the sheltered south side of the terminal building, a phalanx of ten Chusan palms (*Trachycarpus fortuneii*) have been planted, a joke at the expense of tourists who may anticipate more traditional views of Ireland promoted by the tourist industry. The palms are actually associated with 19th-century planting in gardens and parks in the locality.

The serpentine seat draws its inspiration from Gaudí's seat at Parc Güell, the form being both social and sculptural. The entire piece was clad in blue and green swirling and chaotic mosaic by the ceramic artist Orla Kaminska of Tileworks. Although the seat has strong connotations for people in a country whose traditions hold that St. Patrick banished snakes from Ireland, its design is intended to inspire alternative ideas of forms associated with the sea and with travel.

The design intention was to consider the plaza as a 'welcome mat' for the country, conveying all the joy, excitement and anticipation associated with travel, in a place that had more typically experienced the sadness of emigration in a depressed economy.

A market square. One of the most striking design projects to be developed in Ireland coincided

chen Flanken werden von einer 1,50 Meter hohen Mauer begrenzt. So entsteht ein vor den Seewinden geschütztes Mikroklima und die Besucher werden an den Rand des Platzes gelockt, um die Aktivitäten im Hafen und das An- und Ablegen der Fähre zu beobachten.

An der geschützten Südseite des Anlegers entstand eine Reihe von zehn Hanfpalmen (Trachycarpus fortunei) – ein Witz auf Kosten der Touristen, die wohl einen traditionelleren Blick auf Irland erwarten dürften, etwa wie der von der Tourismusbranche propagierte. In Wirklichkeit spielen die Palmen auf Pflanzungen in irischen Gärten und Parks des 19. Jahrhunderts an.

Die geschwungene Bank wurde von der Bank Gaudís im Park Güell inspiriert. Ihre Form ist so gemeinschaftsfördernd wie skulptural. Die Bank wurde von der Keramikerin Orla Kaminska von der Firma Tileworks mit einem chaotisch anmutenden Wirbel aus blauem und grünem Mosaik bedeckt. Sie erinnert die Iren an die Sage, nach der der Heilige Patrick die

Lichtstelen flankieren den Zugang zum Fähranleger in Dun Laoghaire. Der Entwurf für die Keramikmosaikbänke wurde von Gaudís Bank im Parc Güell inspiriert. **Die Sitzelemente in geschwungener Linie erinnern die Iren an die Sage, nach der der heilige Patrick die Schlangen aus Irland vertrieben hat.**

Light steles flank the access to the ferry terminal in Dun Laoghaire. The design of the ceramic mosaic benches was inspired by Gaudí's bench in Parc Güell. **The curving lines of the seating elements remind the Irish of the legend of St. Patrick, who banished snakes from Ireland.**

Ferry Terminal Plaza, Dun Laoghaire
Client: Department of the Marine
Landscape architect: Mitchell and Associates
Design team: Burke-Kennedy Doyle Architects, PH McCarthy and Partners,
Engineers
Area: 6,000 square metres
Winner of the Irish Landscape Institute Design Award 1995

Smithfield, Dublin
Client: Dublin Corporation
Architect: McGarry níÉanaigh Architects
Engineers: Ove Arup and Partners
Size: 1.2 hectares
Cost: IEP 3.5million
Winner of the first European Prize for Urban Public Space awarded by the
Centre de Cultura Contemporània de Barcelona and the Institut Français de
l'Architecture 2000

Die Proportionen des Platzes wurden durch Bänder aus Granitplatten verstärkt, im bestehenden Kopfsteinpflaster verlegt im 45-Grad-Winkel. In Anlehnung an das Pflaster erhalten die Poller einen schrägen Einschnitt. 26 Meter hohe Lichtmasten sind schon von weitem als Teil der Stadtsilhouette sichtbar.

The proportions of the square are emphasised by strips of granite tiles laid out at an angle of 45 degrees to the existing cobblestone paving. The bollards, reflecting the paving, are incised at an angle. The 26-metre-high light masts are visible from afar as part of the town's skyline.

with the millennium celebrations and expresses the confidence and bravado of our cultural climate. The renewal of Smithfield Market in the north inner city of Dublin was a design competition commissioned by the City Corporation in 1997. The brief was simple: 'to establish Smithfield as the major civic space in Dublin City for the 21st century.' Its intention was to provide a flagship development to encourage new investment in a run down quarter and draw economic and cultural activities westward from the city centre.

The scheme reinforces the proportions of the square with an elegant 45-degree angle of granite paving flags crossing the existing cobble set surfacing, and a line of twelve lighting masts, each 26 metres high, topped by gas braziers with flames reaching a further two metres. The lighting of the new square became a dramatic event on the city skyline.

On each mast, a huge galvanised trough houses eight spotlights which reflect off two white powder coated steel sails, each measuring nine square metres, bathing the square in a soft lunar light. The effect is a highly dramatic and emotionally powerful use of light. Rarely is such a unique identity successfully achieved in a place with bespoke lighting elements.

The branding of the space is continued with specially commissioned bollards. The simple stainless steel column is incised at a 45-degree angle alluding to the paving design, and looking like something you might tie your horse to. Further, a special kerb stone marries with the paving, again by reproducing the 45-degree angle as a modular unit.

Smithfield is still scene to the dramatic monthly horse market in which the working-

Die neu gepflasterte Fläche des Fishmarket Squares ist Kernstück einer Kette neuer Fußgängerräume entlang des Flusses Corrib. Die robusten Kalksteinbänke wurden eigens für diesen Ort entwickelt.

The newly paved surface of Fishmarket Square forms the central link of a chain of new pedestrian spaces along the river. The robust limestone benches were tailor-made for the site.

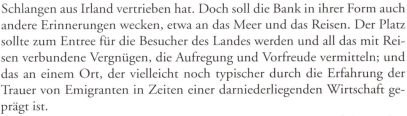

Schlangen aus Irland vertrieben hat. Doch soll die Bank in ihrer Form auch andere Erinnerungen wecken, etwa an das Meer und das Reisen. Der Platz sollte zum Entree für die Besucher des Landes werden und all das mit Reisen verbundene Vergnügen, die Aufregung und Vorfreude vermitteln; und das an einem Ort, der vielleicht noch typischer durch die Erfahrung der Trauer von Emigranten in Zeiten einer darniederliegenden Wirtschaft geprägt ist.

Ein Marktplatz. Der Bau eines bemerkenswerten Platzes fiel mit den Feiern zur Jahrtausendwende zusammen und kann als Ausdruck für das Selbstbewusstsein und das aufgeschlossene kulturelle Klima stehen. Die Neugestaltung des Marktplatzes »Smithfield« in der nördlichen Innenstadt von Dublin ging auf einen Wettbewerb zurück, der 1997 von der City Corporation ausgeschrieben worden war. Die Aufgabenstellung war einfach: Smithfield sollte zum »wichtigsten öffentlichen Raum in der Innenstadt von Dublin für das 21. Jahrhundert« werden. Die Absicht war, ein Aushängeschild zu schaffen, das in einem heruntergekommenen Viertel neue Investitionen anregt und wirtschaftliche und kulturelle Aktivitäten vom Stadtzentrum nach Westen zieht.

Das Konzept betont die Proportionen des Platzes mit einem im eleganten 45-Grad-Winkel verlegten Belag aus Granitplatten, die über das bestehende Kopfsteinpflaster hinwegzulaufen scheinen. Dazu kommen eine Rei-

Fishmarket, Galway
Client: Galway Chamber of Commerce and Industry and Galway Corporation
Design team: Jim Coady and Associates (Architects and Urban Designers), Brady Shipman Martin (Landscape Architects)
Area: 4,000 square metres

he von zwölf 26 Meter hohen Lichtmasten, die von schalenförmigen Gasbrennern gekrönt werden, deren Flammen weitere zwei Meter hoch schlagen. Die Beleuchtung des Platzes wurde zum dramatischen Bestandteil der Stadtsilhouette. Auf jedem Mast befindet sich eine riesige galvanisierte Wanne mit acht Punktscheinwerfern, die von zwei weiß bestäubten, neun Meter im Quadrat messenden Stahlreflektoren verstärkt werden. So wird der Platz quasi in angenehm weiches Mondlicht getaucht. Seine ganz besondere Note bekommt er durch seine individuellen Poller. Eine einfache Säule aus rostfreiem Stahl erhält in Anlehnung an das Pflaster einen Einschnitt in einem Winkel von 45 Grad. Es sieht wie eine Vorrichtung aus, an der man sein Pferd festbinden könnte. Auch bei einem eigens entwickelten Bordstein, der eine Einheit mit dem Pflaster bildet, wurde der 45-Grad-Winkel zum Modul.

Auf Smithfield findet immer noch monatlich der aufregende Pferdemarkt statt, auf dem die Jugendlichen aus der Unterschicht der Stadt ihre Pferde vorführen. Er ist auch Schauplatz einer Reihe von Musikveranstaltungen im Sommer.

Ein Platz am Fluss. Die Stadt Galway auf der anderen Seite des Landes besuchen Touristen auf ihrer Reise durch die dramatischen Landschaften von Connemara, die Karstlandschaft Burren und die Aran-Inseln. Es ist eine Stadt mit regem Kulturleben in den Bereichen Theater und Musik und mit viel Seefahrtsgeschichte. Auf dem Weg zu seiner Mündung in der Bucht von Galway verläuft der Fluss Corrib entlang der Reste der aus dem 16. Jahrhundert stammenden Stadtmauer, die »Spanish Arch« genannt wird und angeblich von Portugiesen erbaut wurde. Sie liegt am Ende der für ihre Bars und Restaurants bekannten und beliebten Quay Street. An diesem Knotenpunkt wurde das erste Projekt eines Gutachtens für diesen Teil der Stadt verwirklicht – der sogenannte Fishmarket Square. Das Gutachten schlug vor, ihn zum Kernstück einer Kette von öffentlichen Fußgängerräumen entlang des Flusses zu machen.

Durch Stufen in Richtung Fluss wird ein leichter Höhenunterschied betont. Die Stufen führen in einen Hain aus Ahorn (Acer pseudoplatanus), der in kreisrunde Baumscheiben aus blauem irischem Kalkstein gepflanzt wurde. Ein Pflasterwechsel im langsam auslaufenden Plattenbelag markiert den Fußweg zur Spanish Arch, die auf der zur Stadt hin gewandten Seite Leuchten und Reflektoren flankieren. Nach Maß gefertigte Sitzgelegenheiten aus Kalkstein säumen die dem Fluss zugewandte Seite des Fußwegs. Der

class youth of the city trade and parade their horses, and is the venue for a series of summer music concerts.

A square next to the river. On the other side of the country, Galway City is the urban destination for tourists visiting the dramatic rural landscapes of Connemara, the karstic Burren and the Aran Islands. It is a culturally active city, with innovative traditions in theatre and music, and a strong maritime history.

The River Corrib flows into Galway Bay, past a remnant of the city walls dating from the 16th century known as the Spanish Arch and allegedly built by the Portuguese, at the end of Quay Street, popular for its bars and restaurants. At this intersection, the space known as Fishmarket Square has been one of the first projects from a study for the urban section of the Corrib to be completed. The proposal was to turn it into a centrepiece for a necklace of public walks along the river.

A subtle change of level is expressed by steps leading towards the river, which feather out into a grove of sycamore (*Acer pseudoplatanus*) set in complicated circular tree grids carved out of blue Irish limestone. The walk towards the Spanish Arch itself is delineated by a change of patterning in the otherwise fanned setts, and flanked by reflective lights to the city side, with bespoke limestone seats lining the river side of the walk. The stone is resistant to vandalism and the seats form a robust item of street furniture, decorating a space that is subject to much boisterous night-time activity. In further projects deriving from the study, the designers have translated the seat form into timber in the quieter residential areas, making a pleasing progression from the urban core.

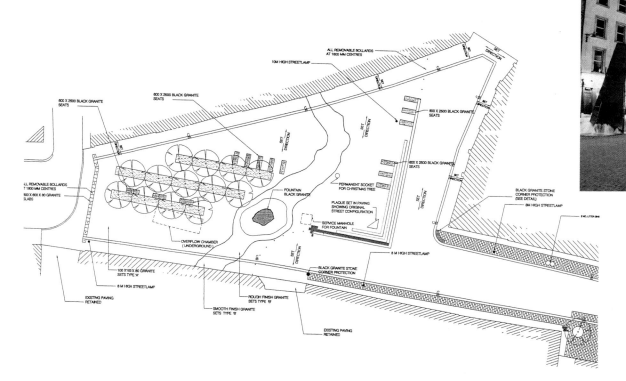

Labels on plan (clockwise and throughout):
ALL REMOVABLE BOLLARDS AT 1800 MM CENTRES
10M HIGH STREETLAMP
800 X 2500 BLACK GRANITE SEATS
800 X 2500 BLACK GRANITE SEATS
800 X 2500 BLACK GRANITE SEATS
800 X 2500 BLACK GRANITE SEATS
SET DIRECTION
PERMANENT SOCKET FOR CHRISTMAS TREE
PLAQUE SET IN PAVING SHOWING ORIGINAL STREET CONFIGURATION
SERVICE MANHOLE FOR FOUNTAIN
FOUNTAIN BLACK GRANITE
OVERFLOW CHAMBER (UNDERGROUND)
ALL REMOVABLE BOLLARDS AT 1800 MM CENTRES
100 X 600 X 80 GRANITE SLABS
8 M HIGH STREETLAMP
EXISTING PAVING RETAINED
100 X100 X 80 GRANITE SETS TYPE 'A'
8 M HIGH STREETLAMP
BLACK GRANITE STONE CORNER PROTECTION
SMOOTH FINISH GRANITE SETS TYPE 'B'
ROUGH FINISH GRANITE SETS TYPE 'B'
EXISTING PAVING RETAINED
8 M HIGH STREETLAMP
BLACK GRANITE STONE CORNER PROTECTION (SEE DETAIL)
8M HIGH STREETLAMP

Für Sitzgruppe und Brunnenskulptur wurde schwarzer indischer Granit verwendet. Wasserstrahlen aus dem kristallförmigen Brunnen spielen ebenso wie ein Band aus spaltrauen Granitplatten an auf einen ehemals existierenden Wasserlauf unterhalb der Platzfläche.

Black Indian granite was used for the group of benches and the fountain sculpture. Water jets from the crystalline shaped fountain refer to a former watercourse under the surface of the square, as does a meander of rcleaved granite setts.

A city square. The most recent new urban space in Ireland is a redevelopment of John Roberts Square at Baronstrand Street in Waterford. The Corporation was planning to lay a new pipeline through one of the principal urban spaces in the city. This gave the opportunity to redesign an otherwise bland space in the shopping quarter of the city.

The square is terminated by a dense grove of oaks (*Quercus rubra*) in three lines. Feathered steps at the opposite end negotiate a small level change, while the main expanse of the space is in plain granite setts, giving a deferential setting to the colour and life of the shop fronts forming the space. A striking crystalline-form sculpture in black Indian granite emerges out of the ground with gushes of water, expressive of a 'lost' watercourse underneath the square. The stream is also expressed by a meandering panel of cleaved black granite setts. Clusters of seats from the same quarry were sculpted at source by the artist, the shape deriving from a sketch by the landscape architect. The design succeeds both as a legible and coherent essay in urban design form, and as a popular city square, with a strong branding expressed in its creative use of exotic stone.

Stein ist resistent gegen Vandalismus und so sind die Bänke eine robuste Straßenmöblierung in einem Stadtraum, in dem nachts viel ungestümes Treiben stattfindet. In weiteren Maßnahmen, die in dem Gutachten vorgeschlagen wurden, haben die Gestalter die Form der Sitzbank in ruhigeren Wohngebieten in Holz wieder aufgenommen und führen so die Entwurfsidee vom Stadtkern aus weiter.

Ein Stadtplatz. Der jüngste Stadtplatz Irlands ist durch die Umgestaltung des John Roberts Square an der Baronstrand Street in Waterford entstanden. Die Verlegung neuer Rohre unter einem der wichtigsten Plätze im Stadtgebiet bot die Chance, einen ansonsten langweiligen Raum in den Einkaufsstraßen der Innenstadt neu zu gestalten.

Am Ende des Platzes steht ein dichter dreireihiger Eichen-Hain (Quercus rubra). In den Platz verlaufende Stufen am gegenüberliegenden Rand bewältigen einen kleinen Höhenunterschied. Der größte Teil des Platzes ist mit einfachen Granitplatten bedeckt, als Rahmen für die Farbenfreude und Lebhaftigkeit der angrenzenden Schaufenster. Aus dem Boden erhebt sich eine eindrucksvolle kristallförmige Skulptur aus schwarzem indischem Granit. Aus ihr schießen Wasserstrahlen, die an einen »verlorengegangenen« Wasserlauf unterhalb des Platzes anspielen, ebenso wie ein mäandrierendes Band von spaltrauen schwarzen Granitplatten. Sitzgruppen wurden aus Stein vom und im selben Granitsteinbruch von der Künstlerin nach einer Skizze des Landschaftsarchitekten geschaffen.

Der Platz ist gut lesbar und ein in sich geschlossenes Beispiel für geglückte Stadtgestaltung – und dazu ein bei der Bevölkerung beliebter Stadtplatz, der durch die phantasievolle Verwendung von exotischem Stein eine eigene Note bekam.

Baronstrand Street, Waterford
Client: Waterford Corporation
Landscape architect: Bernard Seymour Landscape Architect
Design team: Rupert Maddock (City Architect), Eileen McDonough (Sculptor)
Area : 3,000 square metres
Winner of the Irish Landscape Institute Design Award 2000

Kopenhagen – ein interessantes Pflaster

Copenhagen – an interesting beat

Robert Schäfer

Wer nächtens, sagen wir im novemberlichen Sprühregen, in Kopenhagens Hauptbahnhof ankommt und zu Fuß die Innenstadt in Richtung Nyhavn quert, Taxen mißachtend, weil das Hotel geduldig wartet, der hört die Stadt. Vor allem, wenn er einen so praktischen und schicken kleinen Rollkoffer Gassi führt. Was die gummibesohlten Treter nur andeutungsweise den Fußsohlen melden, das rattern die Räder des Samsonite eindringlich ins Ohr: Pflaster allerorten, Steine, Platten und Bänder. Von den 55 000 Menschen, die im Sommer die Fußgängerstraßen bevölkern, jetzt keine Spur. Es wäre ruhig, wäre man selbst nicht unterwegs, wechselnde Rhythmen mit den kleinen Rädern auf den unterschiedlichen Belägen schlagend. Seit dem 17. November 1962 ist die Strøget, eine Kette von Straßen, die die Innenstadt queren, den Fußgängern vorbehalten. Eine der längsten und wohl auch ersten Fußgängerzonen war geboren und erhielt bald Zuwachs mit der Fiolstraede und Købmagergade sowie einigen kleineren Verbindungen, Passagen und der Straedet, in der sich Fußgänger mit Radfahrern und dem motorisierten Verkehr einigen. Doch die Perlen dieser Schmuckkette sind die Plätze, über die auch der nächtliche Spazierweg zwangsläufig führt. Vielleicht kommt im Schein der Lampen der wahre Glanz von Gammeltorv und Nytorv, Amagertorv, Højbro Plads und Gammel Strand noch besser zur Geltung als tagsüber, ganz zu schweigen von den prächtigen Schlußgliedern der Kette, dem Rathausplatz und Kongens Nytorv.

Die ruhige Novembernacht läßt kaum ahnen, daß sich von April bis Oktober vergnügungssüchtige Touristen durch die Strøget schieben und die unzähligen Restaurants und Cafés an Amagertorv und Nyhavn immer überfüllt sind, so daß man sich ob des südländischen Treibens verwundert die Augen reibt, kennt man die Stadt aus den 70ern. Die Fußgängerzone Strøget war arg heruntergekommen, Fastfood-Lokale, Jeansshops und Sexläden dominierten, die Bodenplatten waren gebrochen und Geld für eine Sanierung nicht in Sicht. Dennoch wurden Lösungen verlangt. Unter einem sozialdemokratischen

Innerhalb weniger Jahre wurden die wichtigsten Plätze und Fußgängerbereiche in der Kopenhagener Innenstadt neu gestaltet.
All the major squares and pedestrian zones in downtown Copenhagen were restructured within the space of a few years.

Arriving at the Copenhagen railway station, say in a November drizzle, and walking through the city centre towards Nyhavn, ignoring taxis because a hotel is waiting patiently, you can hear the city. Especially when you are dragging one of those practical and fashionable little carry-on suitcases. What rubber-soled shoes can merely hint to your footsoles, the Samsonite's wheels rattle out insistently: there is paving all over the place, stones, setts and strips. The 55,000 people who populate the pedestrian streets in the summer are nowhere in sight. It would be quiet if you weren't around, beating different rhythms on various pavements with those little wheels.

Ever since 17 November 1962, the Strøget, a sequence of streets crossing the downtown area, has been reserved for pedestrians. One of the longest and probably also first pedestrian zones was born. It multiplied with the addition of Fiolstraede and Købmagergade as well as several smaller links, passageways and the Straedet, where pedestrians and bicyclists join the car traffic. But the pearls on the string are the squares, where your nocturnal walk unavoidably leads. Perhaps the true splendour of Gammeltorv and Nytorv, Amagertorv, Højbro Plads and Gammel Strand is more effective in the lamplight than by day, not to mention the magnificent gems at the ends of the necklace, the town hall square and Kongens Nytorv.

On a peaceful November night you have no idea that pleasure-seeking tourists throng through the Strøget from April to October and that the innumerable restaurants and cafés in Amagertorv and Nyhavn are always overcrowded. It makes you rub your eyes in disbelief at all this southern-looking activity if you recall the

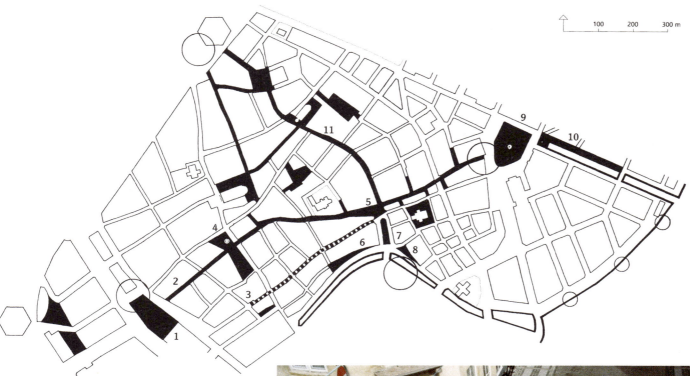

Auf vielen Straßen und Plätzen in Kopenhagens Zentrum haben Fußgänger Vorrang. 1962 wurde Strøget (2) eingeweiht, eine Kette von Straßen, die den Rathausplatz (1) mit Kongens Nytorv (9) und Nyhavn (10) verbindet. An dieser Achse liegen die Plätze Gammeltorv und Nytorv (4), Amagertorv (5), Højbro Plads (7). Weitere Fußgängerbereiche wie die Købmagergade (11), Gammel Strand (6) und Ved Stranden (8) ergänzen das System. Besonders im vergangenen Jahrzehnt konnte der Stadtarchitekt zusammen mit dem Stadtingenieur sukzessive Parkraum in der Innenstadt verdrängen zugunsten von mehr nutzbarem Freiraum. Straedet (3) nennt man eine Verbindung aus drei Straßen, die durch ein guterhaltenes Quartier führt, parallel zur Strøget, aber mit deutlich weniger Passanten. Hier arrangieren sich Fußgänger, Radfahrer und motorisierte Verkehrsteilnehmer. Kreuzungen (Foto rechts) wurden durch kreisförmiges Pflaster aufgewertet, Pflaster mit Granitplatten begrenzen die Verkehrsfläche, die aus Betonplatten besteht.

On many streets and squares in the centre of Copenhagen pedestrians have priority over vehicles of all kinds. Strøget (2) was inaugurated in 1962. It is a sequence of streets connecting the town hall square (1) with Kongens Nytorv (9) and Nyhavn (10). Other squares along this axis are Gammeltorv and Nytorv (4), Amagertorv (5) and Højbro Plads (7). Further pedestrian zones such as Købmagergade (11), Gammel Strand (6) and Ved Stranden (8) complete the network. It was mainly over the last decade that the municipal architect, joined by the municipal engineer, succeeded in gradually supplanting parking areas with more usable free spaces for Copenhagen's residents and its many tourists. Straedet (3) is made up of three streets through a well preserved district and parallel to Strøget, but obviously with fewer pedestrians. Here they must cope with bicyclists and motorised traffic. Intersections (right photo) are highlighted by circular paving. Pavements of granite setts border the road paved with concrete setts.

Straedet
Client: Stadsingeniørens Direktorat Copenhagen
Architects: Stadsarkitektens Direktorat; Sanne Maj Andersen, Thomas Christoffersen
Length: 450 metres
Renovation: 1992

Gammeltorv/Nytorv
Client: Stadsingeniørens Direktorat Copenhagen
Architects: Stadsarkitektens Direktorat; Sanne Maj Andersen, Leif Dupont Laursen
Size: 8,000 square metres
Renovation: 1991 – 1992

Gammeltorv und Nytorv waren früher getrennt durch das Rathaus, das 1795 bei dem großen Stadtbrand von Kopenhagen abbrannte. Bis zur Renovierung 1992 ließen parkende Autos, Mauern, Stadtmöbel verschiedenster Art diesen Stadtraum kaum erkennen. Jetzt sind beide Plätze großzügig verbunden und eine Treppenanlage kennzeichnet den Standort des alten Rathauses. Diese Renovierung wurde von den Benutzern rasch akzeptiert, was der Stadtverwaltung Antrieb gab, die weiteren Platzsanierungen zügig anzugehen.

Gammeltorv and Nytorv used to be divided by the town hall, which burnt down in the great Copenhagen fire of 1795. Until the 1992 renewal, parked cars, walls and all sorts of street furniture all but covered up this urban space. The two squares are now united and spacious. A stairway indicates the site of the former town hall. This reconstruction was soon accepted by the users, giving the municipal administration the impetus to begin renovating the other squares as soon as possible.

city of the 70s. The Strøget pedestrian zone was badly run-down. Fast food joints, jeans shops and sex shops predominated, the paving stones were broken, and there was no money in sight for renewal. Nevertheless, solutions were demanded. With a social democratic mayor, urban renewal could finally start from 1989 on. The maintenance budget was stretched to cover the costs. In a consistent step by step process, cars were excluded from the centre of town. Gammel Strand, the old bank facing the Christiansborg Palace, formerly the fish market until 1957, was free of cars by 1991, Højbro Plads as early as 1986. Up to five percent fewer downtown parking spots a year was the policy made by the municipal en-

gineer responsible. Thus the city was gradually stripped to make room for urban free space. In 1996 the square surrounding the statue of Bishop Absalon, the city's founder, was given a new granite pavement, as well as the Gammel Strand and Ved Stranden areas. These are some of the most beautiful corners of Copenhagen. Though only a few steps from the extremely lively pedestrian zone, the promenade square along the canal is more conducive to contemplation.

The double square Gammeltorv-Nytorv is completely different. The old and the new square comprise Copenhagen's oldest urban space. The old town hall used to divide the two squares, but after the great fire of 1795 it was not rebuilt.

Bürgermeister konnte schließlich ab 1989 mit der Sanierung begonnen werden. Für die Arbeiten wurde der Unterhaltsetat strapaziert. Konsequent fuhr man auch fort, die Autos aus dem Stadtkern zu vertreiben. Gammel Strand, der alte Strand, Schloß Christiansborg gegenübergelegen, bis 1957 Fischmarkt, wurde 1991 autofrei, Højbro Plads bereits 1986. Bis zu fünf Prozent weniger Parkplätze jedes Jahr in der Innenstadt lautet die Salami-taktik des zuständigen Stadtingenieurs, der so Zug um Zug die Stadt frei macht für städtischen Freiraum. 1996 erhielt der Platz rings um das Denkmal des Stadtgründers Bischof Absalon ein neues Granitpflaster, ebenso die Bereiche Gammel Strand und Ved Stranden, die zu den schönsten Ecken in Kopenhagen zählen. Obwohl nur wenige Schritte von der äußerst belebten Fußgängerzone entfernt, geht es an dem Promenadenplatz am Kanal etwas beschaulicher zu.

Ganz anders der Doppelplatz Gammeltorv – Nytorv, der alte und der neue Platz, der älteste Stadtraum Kopenhagens. Das alte Rathaus trennte

Früher diente der Platz als Marktplatz, dann fast nur noch als Parkplatz. Heute orientiert sich der Gammeltorv auf den Renaissancebrunnen „Caritas", der Nytorv auf das klassizistische Stadtgerichtsgebäude von Christian Frederik Hansen (1805 – 1815), im Foto oben rechts. Manche Kopenhagener vermissen allerdings die Bäume, die im Zuge der Sanierung verschwunden sind.

This square used to serve as a market, later almost only as a parking lot. Now Gammeltorv is oriented towards the Renaissance „Caritas" fountain, and Nytorv towards the classicising municipal court building (1805-1815) by Christian Frederik Hansen (top right in the photo). Some Copenhageners miss the trees that disappeared in the course of urban renewal.

Kein richtiger Platz, eher eine Aufweitung der Strøget ist der Amagertorv, ehemals zugestellt mit Bänken, Blumenkübeln und Verkaufsständen. Die Entscheidung, nach Gammeltorv und Nytorv auch diesen Platz neu zu fassen, fiel der Stadt leicht, nachdem die Geschäftsleute der angrenzenden renommierten Häuser sich an den Kosten beteiligten. So konnte der Bildhauer Bjørn Nørgaard einen aufwendigen Teppich aus verschiedenfarbigen Granitplatten im Sternmuster ausführen.

Amagertorv is not a real square but rather a widening of Strøget. It used to be cluttered with benches, flower planters and vending booths. After Gammeltorv and Nytorv, it was an easy decision for the city to redesign this square as well, once sponsors from the surrounding designer shops contributed towards the costs. Thus the sculptor Bjørn Nørgaard was able to execute his intricate carpet with a star pattern of coloured granite setts.

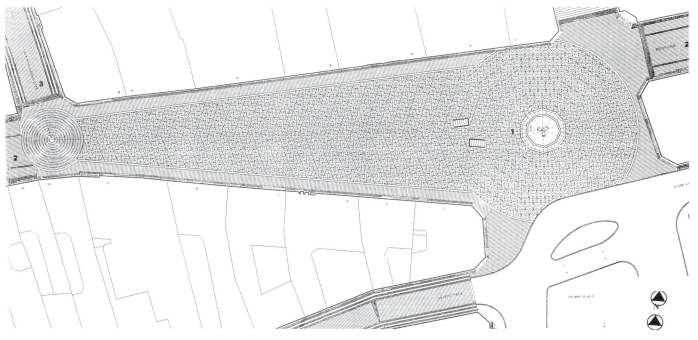

einst beide Plätze, wurde aber nach dem großen Stadtbrand von 1795 nicht wieder aufgebaut. Bis zur Neugestaltung 1992 präsentierte sich der Nytorv als ein mit Autos, Bäumen, Mauern und Mobiliar vollgestellter Platz. Heute ist er leer, eine Treppenanlage markiert den Übergang zwischen beiden Plätzen, an Bäumen zählt der Besucher zwei Linden. Überhaupt keinen am Amagertorv, eher eine Aufweitung der Strøget denn ein echter Platz. Dennoch die gute Stube und äußerst beliebter Aufenthaltsort. Rings um den Storchenbrunnen gruppieren sich Renommiergeschäfte und Straßencafés. Sommers ist der Granitteppich des Künstlers Bjørn Nørgaard dicht belagert. Dank des öffentlichen Interesses am Stadtraum, angestachelt durch die Aufwertung der anderen Plätze, ließen sich für den Amagertorv Sponsoren finden. Für 40 Prozent der Kosten kamen Privatleute auf und so wurden die Pläne ohne Probleme genehmigt, obwohl die Neugestaltung schließlich erheblich teurer geriet als geplant. Nørgaard errechnete am Computer ein Muster für den Belag aus verschiedenen Granitsorten, das dann von italienischen Pflasterern in Präzisionsarbeit verlegt wurde. Stadt-

Until it was redesigned in 1992, Nytorv was full of cars, trees, walls and street furniture. Now it is empty. A stairway complex marks the transition from one square to another, and as for trees, the visitor can count only two lindens. There isn't a single one in Amagertorv, which is more of a widening of Strøget than a true square. Nevertheless it is very presentable and a most popular place to be. Designer shops and sidewalk cafés are grouped all around the stork fountain. In summer the granite carpet by the artist Bjørn Nørgaard is heavily populated. Thanks to public interest in urban space, aroused by the upgrading of other squares, sponsors could be found for Amagertorv. As private donors paid 40 percent of the costs, approval of the plans was no problem even

Amagertorv
Client: Stadsingeniørens Direktorat Copenhagen
Architects: Stadsarkitektens Direktorat; Thomas Christoffersen
Artist: Bjørn Nørgaard
Size: 3,000 square metres
Renovation: 1993

Der Storchenbrunnen kommt auf dem neugestalteten Amagertorv wieder zur Geltung. Als Gegengewicht am anderen Platzende, wo die Niels Hemmingsensgade mündet, schuf der Bildhauer Nørgaard ein rundes Pflastermuster mit einer Kupferplatte in der Mitte sowie einer von innen nach außen verlaufenden Spirale im Pflaster, eine Reminiszenz an das Sonnensymbol in nordischen Steinritzungen.

Im ausgehenden Mittelalter war Amagertorv lebhafter Handelsplatz, unweit der Schiffsanlegestelle am heutigen Højbroplads; heute strömen hier Einheimische wie Touristen zusammen und beleben die Geschäfte wie auch die zahlreichen Cafés. Bei Regen kommt das Pflastermuster besonders gut zur Geltung, bei Sonne ist der Platz so dicht bevölkert, daß das Pflaster kaum ins Auge fällt.

The stork fountain shows to advantage again in the newly designed Amagertorv. As a counterpart on the other end of the square, the sculptor Bjørn Nørgaard created a circular paving pattern. It has a central copper plate and a spiral winding from the inside out in the pavement, recalling the sun symbol on Nordic incised stones.

In the late Middle Ages Amagertorv was the site of lively trade, being near the wharf at what is now Højbro Plads. Today both locals and tourists throng here, livening up the shops and the numerous cafés. The paving pattern is especially effective in the rain; on sunny days the square is so heavily populated that the paving is barely noticed.

though the restructuring ended up being much more expensive than planned. Nørgaard used a computer to calculate a paving pattern of different kinds of granite. It was then laid down by Italian pavers in precision work.

The municipal engineer and the municipal architect work well together, both on the job and personally. One cleared away the cars, the other redesigned the squares. This design project is something the municipal architect Otto Käszner, who has held this position since 1989, would not like to have missed. In his opinion, his department has a competent staff, and the know-how they have acquired by now could not easily be replaced by external planning. "What is a square supposed to be? The ground of the city. Houses provide the life," says Otto Käszner. Hence plain materials are needed, mainly paving. It is not surprising, therefore, that no competitions were held for the design, not giving freelance landscape architects a chance.

The parks department is of course involved and landscape architects also work for the municipal architect. The street furniture is characterized by variety. This is deliberate, because good examples from all periods should be represented in the city. Above all, no design manual. According to Käszner, that has never worked in a live city. Of course the Danish landscape architects were not happy with being ignored in the heart of their capital. They could easily have found room for trees in Højbro Plads or other sites in the stony downtown, and they would have liked to have designed modern benches and wastepaper baskets. Yet criticism of the urban designers' work is not really voiced. Sometimes the distinguished academic council speaks up, a kind of

Der Højbroplads grenzt direkt an Amagertorv. Häuser aus dem 18. Jahrhundert fassen den Platz, auf dem ein Denkmal des Stadtgründers Bischof Absalon steht. Von hier erblickt man die Schloßinsel mit Schloß Christiansborg.

Højbro Plads borders right on Amagertorv. Surrounded by 18th-century houses, the square has a statue of Bishop Absalon, the city's founder. From here there is a view of the island with Christiansborg Castle.

Højbro Plads / Ved Stranden / Gammel Strand
Client: Stadsingeniørens Direktorat Copenhagen
Architects: Stadsarkitektens Direktorat; Sanne Maj Andersen, Leif Dupont Laursen
Size: Højbro Plads and Ved Stranden 9,800 square metres,
Gammel Strand 2,200 square metres
Renovation: 1995 – 1996

ingenieur und Stadtarchitekt arbeiten gut zusammen, von Amts wegen und auch persönlich. Der eine räumt die Autos ab, der andere gestaltet die Plätze neu. Diese Gestaltungsaufgabe möchte sich Stadtarchitekt Otto Käszner, seit 1989 in dieser Stellung, nicht nehmen lassen. Er ist der Ansicht, daß in seiner Abteilung fähige Leute arbeiten würden und das inzwischen erworbene Know-how nicht so leicht zu ersetzen wäre durch externe planerische Leistungen. »Was soll ein Platz sein? Der Boden der Stadt. Die Häuser geben das Leben«, meint Otto Käszner. Einfaches Material sei daher gefragt, vor allem Pflaster. So verwundert es auch nicht weiter, daß für die Gestaltung keine Wettbewerbe ausgelobt wurden und freie Landschaftsarchitekten nicht zum Zuge kommen, obwohl natürlich das Gartenamt beteiligt wird und auch Landschaftsarchitekten in Diensten des Stadtarchitekten stehen. Bei der Stadtmöblierung herrscht die Vielfalt, ganz bewußt, denn gute Beispiele aus allen Epochen sollen im Stadtraum vertreten sein. Bloß keine einheitliche Gestaltung, kein design manual, denn das habe, so Käszner, noch in keiner lebendigen Stadt funktioniert. Selbstverständlich, daß die dänischen Landschaftsarchitekten nicht glücklich über diese Nichtbeachtung im Stadtkern ihrer Hauptstadt sind. Sie hätten durchaus am Højbro Plads oder an anderen Stellen der steinernen Innenstadt Platz für Bäume gesehen und modernere Bänke und Papierkörbe würden sie auch gerne entwerfen. So richtig laut wird diese Kritik an der Arbeit der Stadtgestalter jedoch nicht. Die Stimme erhebt gelegentlich der ehrwürdige Akademierat, eine Art Ästhetikkommission ohne direkte Einwirkungsmöglichkeiten. Akademische Kritik wurde beispielsweise laut im Falle der geplanten Neufassung von Kongens Nytorv, diesem wichtigen Übergang von der mittelalterlichen Stadt zum Stadtteil Frederiksstad, der im 17. Jahrhundert mit einem großzügigen rechtwinkligen Straßensystem angelegt wurde. Hier beginnen oder passieren 15 Buslinien und werktags werden 40 000 Autos gezählt. Die neue Metrolinie nach Amager tangiert den Platz und die Planung sieht eine zweistöckige Tiefgarage für mehr als 800 Autos vor. Dies schien dem Akademierat wohl nicht ausreichend.

Der nächtliche Passant wurde angezogen von einem Lichternetz, das über den Ulmenkranz inmitten des Platzes allzu voradventlich geworfen wurde. Das Flimmern kaschierte das Leiden der Bäume wenigstens nachts, denn mit 80 Jahren waren sie dem Stadtstreß nicht mehr gewachsen. Bei der kompletten Sanierung des Platzes mußten sie Linden weichen, wobei die ovale Form bestehen blieb, wie sie Christian V 1688 um seine Reiterstatue

Ved Stranden und Gammel Strand heißen die beiden Bereiche am Kanal zwischen Schloßinsel und Højbro Plads. Hier wurden die Parkplätze zwischen 1991 und 1995 entfernt. An Gammel Strand, hier befand sich bis in die sechziger Jahre der Fischmarkt, gibt es nun eine Bushaltestelle und Fahrradständer sowie etliche Cafés. Granitpflaster mit Kiesfugen auch hier. Leider arbeiten die modernen Reinigungsmaschinen so effektiv, daß sie die Fugen auskehren – nach einer Lösung dieses Problems wird noch gesucht.

Ved Stranden and Gammel Strand run along the canal between the Castle island and Højbro Plads. Parking was abolished in these two areas between 1991 and 1995. Gammel Strand, the site of the fish market up to the sixties, now has a bus stop, bicycle stands and some cafés. Here too there is granite paving with gravel joints. Unfortunately, street cleaning machines are so thorough that they sweep out the joints. A solution for this problem has not yet been found.

Strøget mündet am Kongens Nytorv, einem verkehrsreichen Platz, der die Altstadt mit dem Stadtteil Fredriksstad verbindet. Als Marktplatz seit 1640 genutzt, wurde der Platz unter König Christian V, dessen Reiterstatue den Platz seit 1688 ziert, angelegt und gepflastert. Erst 1906 entstand die Schmuckanlage in der Mitte, 1916 das charakteristische Baumoval, später kamen noch 130 Parkplätze hinzu – 1989 verschwanden letztere wieder, als die erste Renovierungsphase begann. Ziel für die zweite Phase: eine weite Granitfläche mit dem Baumoval und dem Denkmal in der Mitte, unterkellert von einer mehrstöckigen Tiefgarage.

Strøget ends in Kongens Nytorv. A market square until 1640, it was laid out and paved under King Christian V, whose equestrian statue has graced it since 1688. The central ornamental arrangement dates from 1906, the characteristic oval of trees from 1916. These were later joined by 130 parking spaces, which disappeared again in 1989 when the first renewal phase began. The second phase aims to construct an extensive granite surface, with the tree oval in the middle.

aesthetic commission without direct influence. Academic criticism was heard, for example, concerning the planned restructuring of Kongens Nytorv, the important transition from the medieval town to the Frederiksstad district laid out in the 17th century in a generous orthogonal network of streets. Fifteen bus lines start or pass through here; 40,000 cars are counted on a weekday. The new underground line to Amager stops here and the plan includes a two-storey parkhouse for over 800 cars. Apparently this was not enough for the academic council.

The nocturnal passer-by was attracted by the network of beams of light shining in pre-Advent fashion above the circle of elms in the middle of the square. This flickering concealed the trees' languishing at least by night. At 80 years of age, they could not cope with urban stress any longer. In the complete renewal of the square, they were replaced by linden trees, though still in the oval shape Christian V had laid out around his equestrian statue in 1688 and then replanted by the garden architect Erik Erstad-Jørgensen in 1916. In between, Kongens Nytorv had served as drill ground; the trees were in the way and cut down in 1749.

If the oval of trees on the representative pentagonal square stands for royal Copenhagen, then the other end of the Strøget with the town hall square could characterize the more popular city. Not only because a major northern industrial exhibition took place here in 1888, before the architect Martin Nyrop won the competition for the new town hall, built from 1892 to 1905 in a mixture of Italian and northern styles. It is close to the people not only because the Tivoli amusement park is a few steps away – it was set up on

Kongens Nytorv
Client: Stadsingeniørens Direktorat Copenhagen
Architects: Stadsarkitektens Direktorat;
Leif Dupont Laursen
Size: 25,700 square metres
Renovation: 1992 – 2000

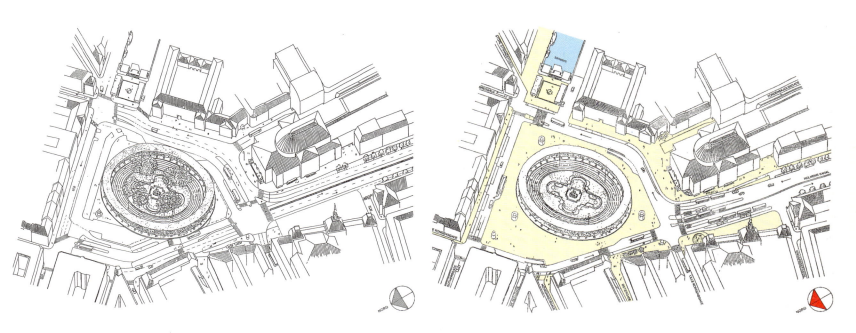

the razed ramparts in 1843 to keep the citizens from starting a revolution. 100,000 Danes celebrated their soccer players here on the town hall square in 1992 when the team won the European championship. The bronze Bishop Absalon over the town hall portal saw the huge crowd that day on a square which at first, after a competition, had been sunken and shaped like a shell, subtly referring to Siena. Later, during the war, it had to cover bomb shelters. Its provisional postwar covering of plain setts served until 1996, when Copenhagen was the Cultural Capital of Europe and naturally needed a town hall square that could be shown off. Under pressure to meet the deadline, the commissioned architecture office KHR A/S, with the consulting collabora-

anlegen ließ und wie sie Gartenarchitekt Erik Erstad-Jørgensen 1916 wiederbegründete. Dazwischen diente Kongens Nytorv als Exerzierplatz, die Bäume störten und fielen 1749. Steht das Baumoval auf dem fünfeckigen repräsentativen Platz für das königliche Kopenhagen, so mag das andere Ende der Strøget mit dem Rathausplatz die volkstümlichere Stadt charakterisieren.

Nicht nur, weil hier 1888 eine bedeutende nordische Industrieausstellung stattgefunden hat, bevor Architekt Martin Nyrop den Wettbewerb für das neue Rathaus gewann, das dann von 1892 bis 1905 im italienisch-nordischen Mischstil entstand. Volksnah nicht nur, weil der Vergnügungspark Tivoli wenige Schritte entfernt liegt – er wurde 1843 auf den geschleiften Wallanlagen errichtet, um die Bürger von Revolutionen abzuhalten. 100 000 Dänen feierten auf dem Rathausplatz ihre Fußballspieler, als diese 1992 Europameister wurden. Der bronzene Bischof Absalon über dem Rathausportal erblickte damals eine riesige Menschenmenge auf einem Platz, der zunächst nach einem Wettbewerb in dezenter Anlehnung an Siena muschelschalenförmig eingetieft ausgeführt war, dann während des Krieges Bunker überdecken mußte. Das Nachkriegsprovisorium, ein einfacher Plattenbelag, diente seinem Zweck bis 1996, als Kopenhagen den Titel Europäische Kulturhauptstadt trug und natürlich einen renommierfähigen Rathausplatz brauchte. Unter Termindruck schaffte es das beauftragte Architekturbüro KHR A/S unter beratender Mitwirkung des Stadtarchitekten, in nur eineinhalb Jahren zu planen und zu realisieren.

Nun führt die Vesterbrogade nicht mehr durch den Platz, der erneut eine sanfte Schalenform erhielt und nun eindeutig dem Rathaus zugeordnet ist. Treppenstufen überwinden den neuen Höhenunterschied, was etwas unmotiviert wirkt. Pflanztröge und Bänke geben auf den schiefen Flächen ein schräges Bild ab. Der Bodenbelag besteht aus Beton und französischem Granit, im Zickzackmuster verlegt. Dem Rathaus gegenüber liegt ein Busbahnhof, der den Platz abschließt, jedoch durch ein modernes Terminalgebäude aus Glas und Aluminium elegant von der weiten Fläche abgetrennt wirkt. An dieser Architektur reiben sich nun Politiker und Bürger mehr als an irgendeiner anderen Planung in Kopenhagen. Das schlichte Gebäude wurde sogar zum Wahlkampfthema und es schien nicht ausgeschlossen, daß sich die Kreise durchsetzen könnten, die bereits 1998 diese Architektur wieder abreißen lassen wollten. Warum bloß? Stadtarchitekt Otto Käszner machte die konservative Haltung der Kopenhagener allem Neuen gegenüber als Ursache aus. Moderne Architektur hat es schwer in Kopenhagen. So läßt sich unschwer ausmalen, daß Architektenwettbewerbe für die renovierten Plätze vielleicht bessere Ideen gebracht hätten, wohl aber auf enorme Realisierungsbarrieren gestoßen wären. Bei aller Freude über das geschlossene Stadtbild in Kopenhagens Kernbereich, über die Plätze, die es den Einwohnern erlauben, ihrem Traum vom mediterranen Leben auch in einem Klima nachzuhängen, das die Hälfte des Jahres Wind, Regen und tristen Himmel bringt, über Plätze, die auch unzählige Touristen anlocken: Die Stadt erneuert sich ringsherum. Es laufen Sanierungsprojekte in Vesterbro, Nørrebro und Islands Brygge, ausgedehnte Neubauprojekte auf ausgedienten Hafenanlagen wie Holmen und Langelinie, ganz zu schweigen von der neuen Ørestad auf Amager, von deren Funktionieren vielleicht die zukünftige Rolle Kopenhagens im europäischen Kontext abhängt, sobald der Verkehr über die Øresundbrücke fließt.

Der Besucher wird sich für die Besichtigung dieser Staträume besser den Frühsommer aussuchen und ein Fahrrad benutzen. Dann lohnt es sich

tion of the municipal architect, managed to plan and realise the project in only a year and a half.

Now Vesterbrogade no longer runs through the square, which was given its shell form again, clearly orienting it towards the town hall. Stairs overcome the difference in levels, looking somewhat unmotivated. The planters and benches look crooked on the sloped surfaces. The paving consists of concrete and French granite laid out in a zigzag pattern. Opposite the town hall is the bus station, closing off the square. But its modern glass and aluminium terminal building is distinguished from the broad area. This work of architecture is more of an object of dispute for politicians and residents than any other planning project in Copenhagen. The plain building was even a campaign issue, and if certain groups prevailed it could be torn down as early as 1998.

Why on earth? The municipal architect Otto Käszner blamed the Copenhageners' extremely conservative attitude to anything new. Modern architecture has a rough time in Copenhagen. It is not hard to imagine that architectural competitions for the renovated squares might have brought in better ideas, but they would have run into enormous obstacles to their realisation. Despite enthusiasm about the consistent urban image of Copenhagen's centre, about the squares allowing residents to live their dream of Mediterranean life even in a climate that offers wind, rain and gloomy skies half the year, about squares that also attract countless tourists: the city is being renewed all around. There are renewal projects in Vesterbro, Nørrebro and Islands Brygge. Extensive new architectural projects are developing in former harbour areas such as Holmen and Langelinie, not to mention the new Ørestad on Amager.

Rådhuspladsen
Client: Stadsingeniørens Direktorat, Magistrat of Copenhagen's 4th department
Architects: KHR AS Arkitekter; Lens Kirk
Advisory board: Stadsarkitektens Direktorat
Renovation: 1995

Der Rathausplatz wird als das Zentrum von Kopenhagen angesehen, groß genug für Kundgebungen, Feiern und offizielle Anlässe, im Kreuzungspunkt vieler Verkehrswege. Das im italienischen Stil gehaltene Rathaus von 1905 erhob sich einst über einer konkav gewölbten Platzfläche. Bei der Neugestaltung griffen die Architekten dieses Motiv wieder auf, so daß man heute über drei Stufen zum Platz hinuntersteigt. Dem Rathaus gegenüber stellten die Architekten ein Terminalgebäude, das den Busbahnhof im nördlichen Teil des Platzes abschirmt. Doch gerade dieses moderne, leichte Glas-Aluminium-Gebäude ist vielen ein Dorn im Auge. Der Belag des Platzes besteht aus Granit- und Betonplatten, 85 000 Stück insgesamt.

The town hall square is considered the centre of Copenhagen. It is large enough for public proclamations, celebrations and official occasions, and at the junction of many traffic arteries. The Italian-style town hall completed in 1905 used to tower over a concave square inspired by Siena. In the new design the architects revived this shape, so that three steps now lead down into the square. Opposite the town hall they placed a terminal building, shielding the bus station in the northern part of the square from view. This modern and light glass and aluminium building is a thorn in the side of many Copenhageners – it may even be torn down. The square's paving consists of granite and concrete setts, 85,000 in all.

The future role of Copenhagen in the European context may depend on whether Ørestad works, once traffic rolls across the Øresund bridge.

The visitor would be better off chosing early summer to view these urban areas and go by bicycle. However, it is worth it to look at two newly made squares now. They are both on Hans Christian Andersens Boulevard: Otto Mønsteds Plads near Langebro, and Jarmers Plads near Ørsteds Park. About one kilometre apart, they each form representative squares in front a bank.

Otto Mønsteds Plads is surrounded by buildings dating from the turn of the century. The Nykredit real estate bank subsidised a limited competition among five artists, won by the Danish sculptor Hein Heinsen for his "Mirror

Otto Mønsteds Plads
Clients: Nykredit AS, Stadtsingeniørens Direktorat
Architects: Stadsarkitektens Direktorat; Sanne Maj Andersen
Artist: Hein Heinsen
Size: 2,500 square metres
Construction: 1996

and Compression". This monolith of polished Swedish granite stands on paving made of two kinds of Bornholm granite, bordered with granite pavement.

Probably the most elegant square in Copenhagen was also the result of a competition. The architecture office Brandt, Hell, Hansted and Holscher created an imposing forecourt for the Realkredit Danmark bank. The construction costs remain a mystery, because the publicised sum of ten million Danish crowns could not even have sufficed for a quarter of the complex. Distinguished and expensive, it was inaugurated in August 1997 and its fame among skateboarders spread like wildfire.

The square relies on few elements and materials. It tops an underground carpark and rests on large granite blocks from Norway. The same granite also forms the benches, into which the lighting is integrated. Marble walls refer to the building. A grove of plane trees breaks up the square. Low spotlights were installed here as well, making all the lighting in this complex below knee level and allowing a glarefree view of Copenhagen's nighttime sky.

The quality of the idea, realisation and material in Jarmers Plads is convincing. It makes the visitor wish for something like it at the entrance to a city.

From there it is not far to the railway station, for whose square no one seems to have any ideas and for whose design there is no sponsor in sight. And so the visitor had better leave the city where he first entered it, pulling his little carry-on up the steps of the side entrance to the station. If he takes one last look back, he can see Tivoli. If that doesn't cheer him up...

aber noch, zwei neu angelegte Plätze anzuschauen, die beide am Hans Christian Andersens Boulevard liegen: Otto Mønsteds Plads in der Nähe der Langebro und Jarmers Plads am Ørsteds Park. Etwa einen Kilometer voneinander entfernt, bilden beide repräsentative Vorplätze für die bedeutenden Institutionen. Der Otto Mønsteds Plads ist von Gebäuden aus der Jahrhundertwende umgeben. Die Bodenkreditanstalt Nykredit finanzierte einen beschränkten Wettbewerb zwischen fünf Künstlern, den Bildhauer Hein Heinsen mit seinem Werk »Spiegel und Verdichtung« gewann. Sein Monolith aus poliertem schwedischen Granit steht auf einem Belag aus zweierlei Bornholmgranit, der von Granitpflaster eingefaßt wird.

Ebenfalls ein Wettbewerb brachte die derzeit wohl eleganteste Platzanlage Kopenhagens. Das Architekturbüro Brandt, Hell, Hansted und Holscher schuf der Kreditanstalt Realkredit Danmark ein repräsentables Entree. Die Baukosten bleiben ein Rätsel, denn die offiziell angeführten zehn Millionen Dänenkronen dürften nur für einen Teil der Anlage gereicht haben. Edel und teuer präsentiert sich, was im August 1997 eingeweiht wurde und sich rasch bei der Skateboardjugend als Übungsgelände herumgesprochen hat. Was im übrigen die Bauherren nicht stört, ist doch ein belebter Platz ein sicherer Platz und jeder Nutzer wertet die Anlage auf. Der Platz kommt mit wenigen Elementen und Materialien aus. Er liegt über einer Tiefgarage und ruht auf großen Granitblöcken aus Norwegen. Aus demselben Granit sind auch die Bänke, in die ein Teil der Platzbeleuchtung integriert ist. Mauern aus Marmor beziehen sich auf das Gebäude. Ein Platanenhain lockert den Platz auf und auch hier sind flache Strahler angebracht, so daß sämtliche Lichtquellen der Anlage unter Kniehöhe liegen, was einen blendfreien Blick auf Kopenhagens Nachthimmel erlaubt, inmitten der Stadt.

Die Qualität von Idee, Ausführung und Material überzeugt am Jarmers Plads und läßt beim Besucher den Wunsch reifen, ähnliches einmal an einem städtischen Entree erleben zu dürfen. Es ist nicht weit von hier zum Bahnhof, für dessen Vorplatz niemand etwas einzufallen scheint und für dessen Gestaltung kein Geldgeber in Sicht ist. So verläßt der Besucher die Stadt lieber wieder dort, wo er sie betreten hat und zieht seinen kleinen Rollkoffer über die Stufen des Bahnhofseiteneingangs. Blickt er sich hier noch einmal um, so sieht er den Tivoli. Wenn das nicht heiter stimmt...

Der Otto Mønsteds Plads konzentriert sich auf eine dominante Skulptur von Hein Heinsen. Das Polizeipräsidium von 1920 als markantes neoklassizistisches Bauwerk dominiert den Stadtraum. Die Dreiecksform des Platzes wurde daher auf dieses Gebäude abgestimmt, Dreiecke kommen auch im Belag aus zwei verschiedenen Bornholm-Graniten vor. Die Skulptur trägt den Namen „Spiegel und Verdichtung" – ein Monolith aus poliertem schwedischem Granit.

Otto Mønsteds Plads revolves around a prominent sculpture by Hein Heinsen. The distinctive neoclassical police headquarters dating from 1920 dominate the space. Hence the triangular shape of the square was based on this building. Triangles also appear in the paving made of two kinds of Bornholm granite. The sculpture is called "Mirror and Compression" – a monolith of polished Swedish granite.

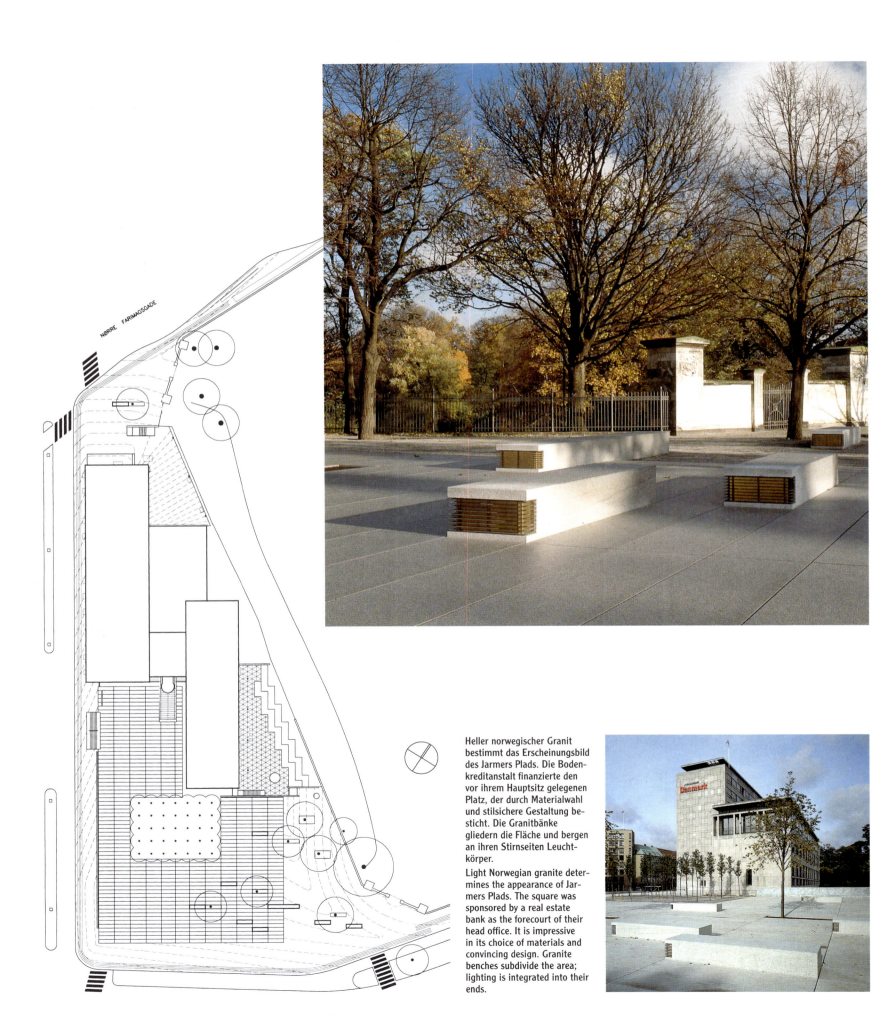

NØRRE FARIMAGSGADE

Heller norwegischer Granit
bestimmt das Erscheinungsbild
des Jarmers Plads. Die Bodenkreditanstalt finanzierte den
vor ihrem Hauptsitz gelegenen
Platz, der durch Materialwahl
und stilsichere Gestaltung be-
sticht. Die Granitbänke
gliedern die Fläche und bergen
an ihren Stirnseiten Leucht-
körper.

Light Norwegian granite determines the appearance of Jarmers Plads. The square was
sponsored by a real estate
bank as the forecourt of their
head office. It is impressive
in its choice of materials and
convincing design. Granite
benches subdivide the area;
lighting is integrated into their
ends.

An der westlichen Seite braust der Verkehr auf dem Hans Christian Andersen Boulevard vorbei, an die östliche grenzt der ruhige Ørstedspark. Es wäre zuviel gesagt, behauptete man, der Jarmers Plads hätte zu den beliebtesten Plätzen Kopenhagens gehört. Dies hat sich mit der Neugestaltung geändert. Ein Architektenwettbewerb sah 1996 das Büro Brandt Hell Hansted und Holscher als Gewinner, die Fachwelt Ende 1997 bereits die fertige Anlage. Der Platz wurde sofort angenommen und belebt, was den Platz auch abends nun zu einem sicheren Ort macht. Sehr großen Wert legten die Architekten auf die Beleuchtung, die niedrig und blendfrei angebracht wurde. Ein Platanenhain ruht inmitten der weiten Granitfläche, zwei Linden sind mehr zum Eingang von der Parkseite her orientiert. Tompak, eine Messing-Kupfer-Legierung, ist das Material für eine elegante »schwebende« Treppe und für die Leuchten. Insgesamt gesehen ein gelungener Platz über der Garage der Bodenkreditanstalt.

On the west, traffic rushes by along Hans Christian Andersens Boulevard, on the east is the quiet Ørsteds Park; no one could have claimed that Jarmers Plads was one of Copenhagen's favourite squares. The new design changed all that. An architectural competition resulted in the Brandt, Hell, Hansted and Holscher office winning the prize in 1996 and by the end of 1997 the professional world could admire the completed square, a gem on the edge of the old city. The square immediately found acceptance and its popularity makes it a safe place even at night. The architects paid a lot of attention to the lighting, installed at a low level and glare-free. A plane tree grove reposes in the midst of the broad granite expanse; two linden trees are oriented towards the entrance on the park side. The elegant "floating" stairway and the lamps are made of Tompak, a brass and copper alloy. All in all, this square atop the real estate bank's underground carpark is successful, probably the most beautiful newly designed free space in Copenhagen.

Jarmers Plads
Client: Realkredit Danmark
Architects: Brandt Hell Hansted Holscher Arkitekter; Erik Brandt Dam;
Competition: 1996
Construction: 1997

Universitätsplatz Tromsø, Norwegen

The university square of Tromsø, Norway

Bjarne Aasen

Die Universität von Tromsø ist die nördlichste Universität der Welt: Sie liegt auf 70 Grad nördlicher Breite. Dank der Mitternachtssonne sind die Sommernächte hell. Im schneereichen Winter herrscht dagegen vom 21. November für zwei Monate die dunkle Polarnacht. In dieser Zeit taucht die Sonne nicht über dem Horizont auf. Klima, Natur und Kultur dieses subarktischen Teils von Norwegen bestimmten den Entwurf für den Campus der Universität. 1988 wurden fünf Künstler zu einem beschränkten Wettbewerb eingeladen, und Guttorm Guttormsgaards Labyrinth fand den Zuspruch der Jury.

Ich war als Landschaftsarchitekt Mitglied der Jury und wurde dann vom Bauherrn, der Universitätsverwaltung, gebeten, an der Ausführung mitzuwirken. Die Grundidee einer labyrinthischen Schlange geht aus der arktischen Mythologie hervor, wo sie als magisches Symbol vor fremden Mächten oder Geistern schützen soll. Vor der Universität umschließt sie eine warme, leuchtende Quelle.

Es gab keine besonderen Anforderungen an die Gestaltung des Platzes. Er sollte jedoch nutzbar sein für die 7000 Studierenden und Angestellten der Universität. Außerdem wurde Wert darauf gelegt, daß die Baumaterialien aus Nordnorwegen kommen und daß die Anlage von Nordnorwegern ausgeführt wird. Speziell ausgesuchte Steine, von Kies bis zu von Wasser und Eis geschliffenen Geröllbrocken, wurden mit geschnittenen und polierten Steinen zusammengefügt und in Mustern innerhalb des Labyrinths verlegt. Das Wasserbecken in der Mitte verbindet die Erde mit dem Himmel. Aus dem polierten, spiegelnden Stein quillt das heiße Wasser. Im Winter bildet

In early 1988, five artists were invited, in a limited competition, to submit ideas for the form and shape of the whole of the University Square around which are located the main buildings of Tromsø University. A year later, Guttorm Guttormsgaard's proposal for a labyrinth, with a central feature of a hot-water spring, was accepted as the winning scheme. There has been little change since then from the ideas submitted for the competition. Bjarne Aasen, a member of the competition jury, was asked by the University of Tromsø to collaborate in the implementation of the scheme.

Tromsø is the most northerly university in the world, on latitude 70 degrees North, and, for a period of exactly two months from 21 November, the polar night sets in and the sun never rises above the horizon. But the dark snowy winters give way to light summers with the unrivalled beauty of the midnight sun. For staff, students and the local population, surrounding natural elements and the forces of nature are very evident and a real part of everyday existence. It is both appropriate and practical that the designer turned to this recurring theme. A labyrinthine snake surrounds and guards a symbolic, warm, luminous source in the centre. The idea of the labyrinth pattern here stems from Arctic folklore which is one of the youngest labyrinth cultures in the world. The labyrinths were probably formed as a magical symbol to protect communities against external forces.

It was very important to all concerned that this design for the University Square should be constructed by people from northern Norway, using local skills and materials. Specially selected stones in all sizes, from gravel and natural occur-

Klima, Natur und Kultur des hohen Nordens spiegeln sich in den Außenanlagen und dem Brunnen der Universität Tromsø wider.

The climate of the Far North and its nature and culture are reflected in the outdoor facilities at the University of Tromsø.

Zur Gestaltung des Universitätsplatzes von Tromsø wurde 1988 ein Wettbewerb ausgeschrieben, den der norwegische Künstler Guttorm Guttormsgaard gewann. Zusammen mit dem Landschaftsarchitekten Bjarne Aasen realisierte er eine labyrinthische Bodengestaltung, die eine warme Quelle umschließt. Licht strahlt aus 4000 Öffnungen im Boden und symbolisiert den sternengesprenkelten Polarhimmel. Da der Boden viele Wochen im Jahr gefroren ist, wurde eine unterirdische Heizung angelegt. So können die 7000 Studierenden und Angestellten der Universität auch im Winter das Wasser- und Lichtspektakel erleben.

The Norwegian artist Guttorm Guttormsgaard won the competition held in 1988 to find designs for the university square in Tromsø. In collaboration with the landscape architect Bjarne Aasen, he created a labyrinth-like design for the paving that surrounds a warm spring. Light shines out from 4,000 openings in the ground, reflecting the star-studded skies of the long polar nights. Since the ground is frozen hard for many months, an underground heating system enables students and university employees to enjoy the interplay of water and light even in winter.

Client: University of Tromsø, Directory of Public Construction and Property,
Foundation for New Public Building Decoration
Design: Guttorm Guttormsgaard, artist; Bjarne Aasen, landscape architect
Landscape gardener: Roar Markussen
Drawings: Peter Aasen, architect
Construction period: 1989–1991
Size: 3000 square metres
Costs: Nkr 3 800 000

Vegetation spielte bei der Gestaltung des Universitätsplatzes von Tromsø keine große Rolle. Lediglich Zwerg- und Polarbirken wurden in der Gegend entnommen, Fichten und Kiefern stammen aus nordnorwegischen Baumschulen. Kies, geschliffene Geröllbrocken und polierte Steine bilden ein labyrinthisches Muster um den zentralen Brunnen.

Vegetation does not play an overly great role in the design for the square at Tromsø University, with solely local dwarf and polar birches being used along with fir and pine trees from north Norwegian tree nurseries. Gravel, cut polished stones and scree worn smooth by the action of water and ice form a labyrinth-like pattern around the spring.

Selbst unter der winterlichen
Schneedecke sind die
niedrigen Stufen des Labyrinths noch zu erkennen.
Wie eine Schlange winden
sich Kreisbögen um den Brunnen, dessen heißes Wasser
den Schnee schmelzen läßt.

The ridges of the labyrinth
can even be made out under
the snow, which the warm
water melts away in the prox-
imity of the spring.

ring shingle, to errant boulders ground by ice or shaped by water, have been joined with cut, honed and polished stones and placed in intricate patterns within the overall labyrinth. The centrally placed basin conjures up the immediacy of earth and sky. From within the polished, mirror finish, hot water creates frost 'smoke' in winter and in summer is suggestive of warmer climates further south. Illumination from a light source at the bottom of the basin streams out into the darkness from 4000 holes, to symbolize the star-studded northern polar sky. Aware that for many weeks of the year the ground is frozen and snow-covered, we have installed underground heating to melt the snow and ensure that the central feature is always visible and active, even in the depths of winter.

Vegetation has little place in this composition, corresponding to the Arctic character of the surrounding area. But small Arctic birches have been collected from nearby and spruce and pine brought in from nurseries in northern Norway.

Sculptures by the Lapp artist Anne Lise Josefsen have been added to this unusual landscape design. The whole project has been made possible through the cooperation of Tromsø University and the Norwegian Fund for Art in State Buildings. The designer has turned the apparent adversity of the severe climate into a powerful, positive force, forging a highly symbolic and fascinating statement out of what might otherwise have been an alienating experience. Reliance on local crafts, labour, and materials has, one feels, reflected many of the values in this community. In its own way, the labyrinth theme responds to the local atmosphere and creates a vivid sense of place – highly appropriate to a university.

sich Frostnebel, und im Sommer erinnert es an wärmere Klimabereiche im Süden. Eine Lichtquelle am Grund des Beckens sendet ihre Strahlen durch 4000 Öffnungen in die Dunkelheit und symbolisiert den sternengesprenkelten Polarhimmel. Da der Boden viele Wochen im Jahr gefroren und schneebedeckt ist, verlegen wir eine unterirdische Heizung, um den Schnee zu schmelzen und sicherzugehen, daß das Wasser- und Lichtspektakel auch im tiefsten Winter zu erleben ist. Die Vegetation spielt naturgemäß in diesen nördlichen Breiten keine besonders große Rolle. Zwerg- und Polarbirken wurden in der Gegend entnommen und rund um den Universitätsplatz eingesetzt, Fichten und Kiefern stammen aus nordnorwegischen Baumschulen. Skulpturen der samischen Künstlerin Anne Lise Josefsen ergänzen diese etwas ungewöhnliche Anlage, die durch die Unterstützung des Norwegischen Fonds für Kunst an staatlichen Gebäuden möglich wurde.

Der Entwurf übertrug die Strenge des nordischen Klimas in eine höchst symbolische und ausdrucksstarke Gestaltung, die sich ideal der universitären Atmosphäre anpaßt. Studierenden und Angestellten der Universität Tromsø bedeuten die Naturgewalten viel; sie sind Teil ihres Alltags.

Das heiße Wasser des Brunnens quillt aus einem polierten, spiegelnden Stein in der Mitte des Universitätsplatzes von Tromsø. Die Schlange ist Vorbild für die labyrinthische Platzgestaltung; sie taucht auch als Motiv auf dem Brunnenrand auf. In der arktischen Mythologie gilt sie als magisches Symbol, das Schutz vor fremden Mächten oder Geistern bietet.

The warm water of the spring wells up out of a polished, shining stone placed at the centre of Tromsø's university square. The labyrinth-like design is based on the symbol of the snake, which is also used to decorate the stone where the spring emerges. In Arctic mythology, the snake is regarded as a magic symbol that provides protection from unknown forces and spirits.

Geometrie und Gefühle

Geometries and feelings

Poble Nou, near the sea on the northern periphery of Barcelona, is one of those districts undergoing a thorough urban renewal. Developing on the site of a former paper factory is a new urban structure with wide streets and housing in the centre of the district. In addition, it is hoped that public spaces will be turned back into open spaces that can be intensively used. One of these is Julio González Square, positioned like a navel between the rigid rectangular grid of the Cerdá urban expansion and the old, early 19th-century urban structure parcelled out in small lots. As unusual as the morphology of the district around it are the dimensions of the site: too small for a park and too big for a garden, it comes closest to being a square.

Under these conditions, it has now developed into a place that is considered safe, open, independent and, in a modest way, even spectacular. Its musical score of vistas, low walls, water channels, convexities and slopes in harmony with the materials creates a complex melody of levels, colours and structures. On the ground level it is a composition of lawns, crushed stone, earth, clay chippings, gravel, pavement, stone and concrete setts as well as granite. On the level above, the music is played by the alternating colours and perfumes of plane trees, carob, pepper and mulberry trees, of pines, laurels, tamarinds and acacias, of tipuana, Judas-trees and bombacacea trees, as well as of poplars and palm trees.

There are thus two underlying conceptual approaches that intersect and accompany each other on the Julio González square. They meet, separate and find their way together again, just as the changes and moods of life like to do. For the shadows and light, the fruits, leaves and colours,

Poble Nou liegt nahe zum Meer an der nördlichen Peripherie von Barcelona und ist eines der Quartiere, in denen die Stadt von Grund auf erneuert wird. Dort, wo früher die alte Papierfabrik stand, entwickelt sich heute mit großen Straßen und dem Wohnungsbau im Zentrum des Quartiers eine neue Stadtstruktur. Zudem erhofft man sich, öffentliche Stadträume als Freiraum zurückgewinnen und intensiv nutzen zu können. Ein Beispiel dafür ist der Platz Julio González: Er liegt wie ein Nabel zwischen dem starren Quadratraster der Stadterweiterung von Cerdá und der alten, kleinflächig parzellierten Stadtstruktur aus der Zeit zu Beginn des 19.Jahrhunderts. So eigenwillig wie die Morphologie des Quartiers um ihn herum sind auch seine Abmessungen: Für einen Park zu klein und für einen Garten zu groß, ist er am ehesten noch ein Platz.

Mit diesen Vorgaben ist dort nun ein Raum entstanden, der als sicher, offen, lehrreich, eigenständig und auf bescheidene Weise sogar spektakulär gilt. Seine Partitur aus Fluchten, Mäuerchen, Wasserrinnen, Wölbungen und Böschungen ergibt im Zusammenspiel mit den Materialien eine komplexe Melodie aus Ebenen, Farben und Strukturen. Auf Bodenniveau ist das eine Komposition aus Rasen, Schotter, Erde, Tonsplitt, Kies, Pflaster, Stein- und Betonplatten sowie Granit; eine Ebene darüber spielen die wechselnden Farben und Düfte der Platanen, Johannisbrot-, Pfeffer- und Seidenbäume, der Pinien, Lorbeerbüsche, Tamarinden und Akazien, der Tipuana-, Judas- und Flaschenbäume sowie Pappeln und Palmen die Musik.

Es sind also zwei konzeptionelle Grundhaltungen, die sich auf dem Platz Julio González schneiden und begleiten, sich begegnen, trennen und wiederfinden – ganz so, wie es dem Lauf und den Launen des Lebens gefällt. Denn aus dem Schatten und Licht, aus Früchten, Blättern und Farben, aus Wasser und Spuren ergeben sich immer wieder überraschende Bilder. Und natürlich auch aus Gegensätzen wie Betonwürfeln, Bänken, Lichtsäulen, Spielelementen und Menschen.

Beschreibung des Projekts. Der Platz gliedert sich in sieben Teilabschnitte; diese liegen wie Tafeln nebeneinander, sind unterschiedlich lang und jeweils 24 Meter breit. Ihre Oberfläche ist leicht gewölbt – mit den Hochpunkten in der Mittellinie und den Tiefpunkten entlang der Seiten. Je nach Art des Belages und deren Position auf dem Platz gibt es bei den Höhen und Wölbungen drei

Jordi Bellmunt Chiva
Xavier Andreu Barrera

Eine Melodie aus Ebenen, Farben und Strukturen – das ist der Platz Julio González im Quartier Poble Nou.

A melody composed of levels, colours and structures: Julio González Square in the Poble Nou district.

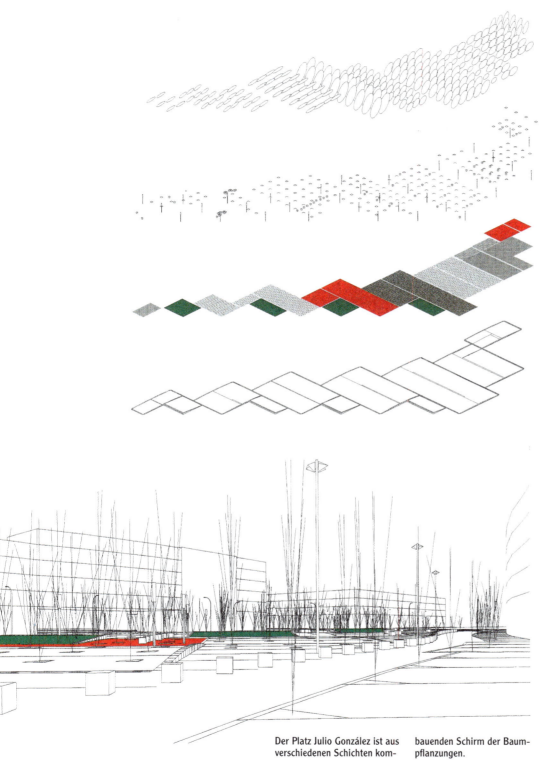

Der Platz Julio González ist aus verschiedenen Schichten komponiert (von unten nach oben): der Grundgeometerie der sieben parallel liegenden Teilflächen, den verschiedenen Bodenbelägen, dem orthogonalen Raster baulicher Elemente sowie dem darauf aufbauenden Schirm der Baumpflanzungen.
Darunter: Perspektive aus Sicht der Fußgänger, vom internen Erschließungsweg aus gesehen.
Rechts: Zwei langgestreckte neue Wohnzeilen fassen das farbige Patchwork des Platzes.

Julio González Square is composed of different layers (from below): the underlying geometry of the seven parallel sections, the different kinds of ground surfacing, the orthogonal grid of structural elements, and the umbrella of tree plantings built up on top.

Below: View from a pedestrian's perspective, seen from the pathway through the square.
Right: Two long, new residential blocks flank the colourful patchwork of the square.

Die Rechtecke der Belag-
flächen sind im orthogonalen
Raster mit Bäumen, Beton-
würfeln und Lampen gegliedert und überstellt.
Seite 17: Die einzelnen Teilflächen sind leicht konvex gewölbt und an ihren Stirnseiten
von kleinen Granitmauern ge-
faßt (oben und Mitte). In den
durchlaufenden Belagflächen
sind die Baumscheiben eher
Aussparungen symbolischer
Art (unten).

The rectangles of the ground
surfacing are subdivided and
superimposed by the orthogonal grid of trees, concrete
cubes and lamps. Page 17:
The individual sections have
slightly convex surfaces and
their front ends are framed by
low granite walls (above and
centre). The beds around the
trees form gaps of a symbolic
kind in the continuous series
of surfaces (below).

the water and various traces keep producing surprising effects. The opposites in the form of concrete cubes, benches, lamp posts, play elements
and people do the same.

Project description. The square is subdivided
into seven sections, lying side by side like panels.
They vary in length and are each 24 metres wide.
Their surfaces undulate slightly, with the highest
points along their central line and the lowest
along their sides. Depending on the type of surface and the section's position in the square, there
are three variants of undulations. The axes dividing the sections are open gutters made of precast
concrete elements. Their function is to drain off
the rainfall. There are four kinds, depending on
what the section's surface is made of.

At the front ends of the seven sections are low
granite walls. They are 40 centimetres wide, their
facades curving the same way as the undulations
of the surfaces they stand in front of. Low granite
walls also frame the four rectangular lawns running towards the footpath along Calle Bilbao.
Their smooth stones rise at a slight incline from
the gutters to a height of 50 centimetres.

A second geometrical pattern on the square is
formed by the surfaces. Rectangles of different
materials are arranged such that each kind of surface extends across two sections, whose central
line in turn separates the different kinds of surfaces. They are linked by precast concrete bands
along which one can walk and run around the
square on one level.

With the exception of two clinker surfaces,
most of the covers are water-absorbent. In order
to be preserved, they have been sunk eight centimetres below the level of the paved surfaces and
the tops of the walls around them.

Plaza Julio González
Site: *Poble Nou, Barcelona*
Client: *Municipality of Barcelona, ICOSA Realties AG*
Design: *Jordi Bellmunt Chiva, architect; Xavier Andreu Barrera, architect;*
Emilio Asensi López
Collaborators: *Anna Zahonero, biologist; Carlos Fuente, C.C.P. engineer*
Planning: *1992; Construction: 1996*
Area: *20,400 square metres*
Costs: *ESP 160,000,000 (EUR 970,000)*

The square's third design element consists of the trees. They have been planted in an orthogonal grid superimposed on the underlying geometry of the rectangles. The different groups vary according to habit, colour and seasonal aspects. The beds around the trees are gaps of a symbolic kind in the continuous series of surfaces.

Benches, fountains and a children's playground complete the park's furniture. It includes precast concrete cubes in different designs and arrangements fulfilling various functions. They are suited for seating and play, and serve as bollards along the access road and elsewhere as sidemarker lights. They thus form part of the square's lighting, which is variable. While seven- and twelve-metre-high lamp posts line the roads, rows of 3.5-metre-high ball lamps between the groups of trees complete the tree plantings with a man-made forest of posts.

Varianten. Die Achsen zwischen den Teilflächen sind offene Rinnen aus vorgefertigten Betonelementen und haben die Funktion, die Niederschläge abzuleiten. Abhängig vom Belag gibt es dabei vier Ausführungsvarianten.

Die Stirnseiten der sieben Teilflächen sind mit kleinen Mauern aus Granit versehen. Sie sind 40 Zentimeter breit und zeigen in der Ansicht die gleiche Krümmung wie die konvex gewölbten Flächen, vor denen sie stehen. Kleine Granitmauern rahmen auch die vier rechteckigen Rasenflächen, die zum Fußweg an der Calle Bilbao hin liegen. Ihre glatten Steine steigen mit sanfter Neigung von den Wasserrinnen bis auf eine Höhe von 50 Zentimeter. Ein zweites geometrisches Grundmuster auf dem Platz sind die Beläge. Es sind Rechtecke aus verschiedenen Materialien. Sie sind so angeordnet, daß jede Einzelfläche sich über zwei Teilflächen erstreckt, wobei deren Mittellinie wiederum die unterschiedlichen Beläge trennt. Verbunden über vorgefertigte Betonbänder kann man auf dem Platz ohne Höhenunterschiede herumlaufen und -spazieren. Mit Ausnahme von zwei Klinkerflächen besteht der überwiegende Teil der Beläge aus wassergebundenen Decken. Um sie auf Dauer zu erhalten, liegen diese acht Zentimeter tiefer als die Pflasterbeläge und die sie rahmenden Mauerkanten.

Drittes Gestaltungselement auf dem Platz sind die Bäume. Sie sind in einem orthogonalen Raster über die Grundgeometrie aus Rechtecken gepflanzt. Die verschiedenen Gruppen sind nach Habitus, Farben und saisonalen Aspekten unterschieden. Die Baumscheiben sind dabei Aussparungen eher symbolischer Art in den durchlaufenden Belagflächen.

Bänke, Brunnen und ein Kinderspielbereich ergänzen die Ausstattung des Platzes. Dazu zählen auch vorgefertigte Betonwürfel, die unterschiedlich gestaltet und plaziert sind und dabei mehrere Funktionen erfüllen: Sie eignen sich zum Sitzen und Spielen, dienen entlang der geschwungenen Erschließungsstraße als Poller und an anderen Stellen als Positionsleuchten. Sie sind damit Teil der Beleuchtung des Platzes, die variabel gehalten ist: Während entlang der Straßen sieben beziehungsweise zwölf Meter hohe Mastleuchten stehen, sind auf dem Platz reihenweise 3,5 Meter hohe Kugelleuchten zwischen die Baumgruppen gesetzt und komplettieren so die Baumpflanzungen mit einem gebauten Stangenwald.

Höfe, Terrassen, Passagen – Kulturzentrum in Gibellina

Courts, terraces and passages for a culture centre in Gibellina

Case Di Stefano heißt das große Landgut im sizilianischen Gibellina, das längst im Verfall begriffen war, als 1968 die Erde bebte und alle wichtigen Dörfer des Belice-Tals zerstörte. Kurz nach dem Erdbeben wurde die Stadt Nuova Gibellina aus dem Boden gestampft, und Anfang der achtziger Jahre entschieden, daß im nahegelegenen Gut Case Di Stefano ein Museum und ein Kulturzentrum für die neue Stadt eingerichtet werden sollten. Denn das Gut hatte die Ländereien rundum verloren und diente somit nicht mehr als Zentrum landwirtschaftlicher Aktivitäten. Als wir den Auftrag erhielten, das Gut zu rekonstruieren und umzubauen, war nicht viel mehr von der ursprünglichen Baumasse übrig als einige verfallene Gebäude und mühsam zu entziffernde Fundamente.

Man muß sich das Gut – nach seinem letzten Besitzer »Di Stefanos Häuser« genannt – als typisches sizilianisches Anwesen mit Doppelhof vorstellen. Hoch über den Ländereien gelegen, die von hier aus bewirtschaftet und verwaltet wurden, machte es den Eindruck einer Festung. Das Zentrum des Guts bildete ein riesiger Hof mit Gefälle, »baglio« genannt, den hangaufwärts das größte der Lagerhäuser begrenzte, und hangabwärts ein niedriges Gebäude mit Räumen für die Verwaltung. An den abfallenden Seiten des Hofes befanden sich, ebenfalls abfallend gestaffelt, eine Reihe von Remisen für landwirtschaftliche Nutzfahrzeuge und die Wohnstätten für das ständige Personal. In der Mitte des »baglio« stand das

Roberto Collovà

Wiederaufbau nach dem Erdbeben: Freiräume und Gebäude des sizilianischen Landgutes Case Di Stefano erhalten eine neue Ordnung.
Renewal after the earthquake: At a landed estate in Sicily, buildings and spaces have been reorganised to create a culture centre.

Case Di Stefano is the name of what was once a large landed estate outside the town of Gibellina in west Sicily. By the time an earthquake shook the region in 1968, destroying all the main villages in the Belice valley, the estate was already decimated and lying in ruins. Shortly after, the authorities built up a new town – Nuova Gibellina – and at the beginning of the eighties, it was decided to set up a museum and culture centre at the nearby estate, which no longer served any concentrated agricultural purpose. When we were commissioned with reconstructing the old buildings, there was very little left of them, except a few ruins and half-buried foundations.

The estate itself – named "Di Stefano's Houses" after its last owner – was typical of Sicilian landed estates in that a divided central yard split the manor and farm buildings into two sections.

Located high on a slope above the demesne as a whole, the manor made the impression of a citadel, and was the centre of estate life. The central yard, known as the *baglio*, was enclosed at its upper end by a large barn and at the bottom by a long, low building with administration rooms. A series of sheds for implements and housing for the farm hands were lined up on the sides. The manor house was set in the middle of the *baglio*, dividing it into an upper and lower section, the former equipped with wells, shelters for farm vehicles and an entrance of its own, and the latter reserved for family use, whereby both were connected by turreted passages and paths. Stock was kept in a smaller yard next to the *baglio*.

In keeping with old Sicilian tradition, the manor also had a purely ornamental garden, set off distinctly from the rest of the buildings, and

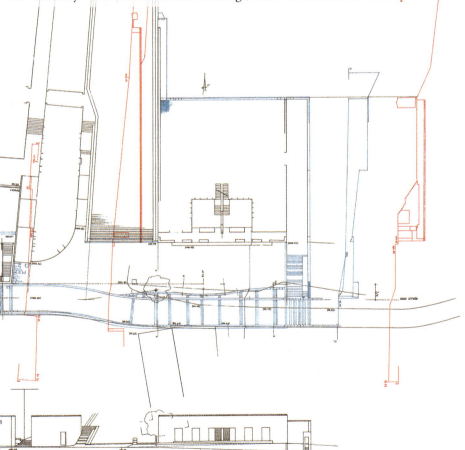

Der Zufahrtsweg aus gestampfter Erde führt zum Werkstattgebäude des umgebauten Landguts. Sich verdichtende Streifen aus weißem Travertin zeigen Gebäude-Eingänge und abzweigende Wege an. Die gebogene Mauer umschließt einen kleinen Garten für die Bibliothek. Dahinter gelangen die Besucher über einen ansteigenden Weg in den Gebäudekomplex. Links: Travertin-Pflaster im Freiraum (blau), innere Gebäudeerschließung (schwarz), Geländeschnitte (rot).

An access path of pounded earth leads up to the workshop building of the converted manor house complex. Stripes of white travertine focus on the entrances to buildings and turning paths. Behind the little library garden, enclosed behind the curved wall, a path leads visitors up to the building complex. Left: Outdoor travertine paving (blue), corridors (black) and cross-sections (red).

Die Besonderheit des oberen Hofes der Case Di Stefano: sein starkes Gefälle, akzentuiert durch Bänder aus weißem Travertin. Wasserrinnen unterbrechen die strenge Geometrie, Flußkiesel füllen die Rasterflächen aus. Durch den Bogen unter dem Aussichtsturm gelangt man auf den Erschließungsweg, über eine Passage durch das Herbergsgebäude auf den unteren Platz.

The distinguishing feature of the upper court at Case Di Stefano is the steep gradient, which the architects accentuated with strips of white travertine and a grid filled with fields of river pebble stones. Diagonal water rills dissect the austere geometry of the court. The arch in the outlook tower leads through to the narrow access path, and a passage in the hostel to the lower court.

Ein schmaler Weg führt zwischen den schlichten Steinfassaden der wiederaufgebauten Gebäude hügelan. Ebene Partien sind mit Platten aus Travertin gepflastert, Treppen und Rampenstufen aus massiven Blöcken aufgebaut. Links im Bild das Werkstattgebäude, rechts die Bibliothek.

A narrow path leads uphill between the simple stone facades of the refurbished buildings. Level areas are paved in slabs of white travertine, while the steps and ramps consist of solid travertine blocks. The workshop building can be seen to the left and the library to the right.

Traditionelle weiß-grüne Kacheln bedecken die Dachterrasse des Servicegebäudes der Case Di Stefano. Da das Gebäude in den Hang gebaut ist, bietet seine Terrasse einen direkten Zugang zum angrenzenden Olivenhain.

Traditional green and white tiles cover the roof terrace of the service building built into the slope at Case Di Stefano, which leads over to an adjacent olive grove.

Den geschlossenen Charakter des ehemaligen Landgutes wollten die Architekten nicht bewahren. Heute eröffnen sich den Besuchern immer wieder Blicke in die sizilianische Landschaft, hier vom unteren Hof aus. Entlang der Werkstätten besteht der Hof aus gestampfter Erde. Links im Bild: der Erschließungsweg, der Eingang zum Bibliotheksgarten.

The architects did not want to retain the formerly closed character of the old manor and farm building complex, with the result that visitors can now catch frequent glimpses of the Sicilian landscape, seen here from the lower court. In the workshop area, the ground consists of pounded earth. To the left of the picture: the access path and the entrance to the library garden.

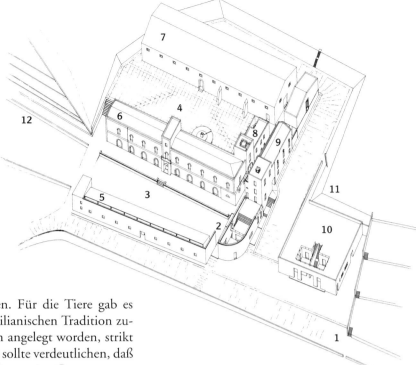

herrschaftliche Haus und teilte den Hof in einen unteren und einen oberen Teil: Der untere Freiraum blieb der Familie vorbehalten, der obere diente der Landwirtschaft und besaß einen eigenen Eingang mit Brunnen und Wetterdach für die Fahrzeuge. Unterer und oberer Hof der Case Di Stefano standen über verschiedene Passagen miteinander in Verbindung; kleine Türme markierten Durchgänge und Eingänge zu den Höfen. Für die Tiere gab es kleinere Höfe neben dem »baglio«. Einer alten sizilianischen Tradition zufolge war neben dem Landgut ein Schmuckgarten angelegt worden, strikt von dem Gebäudekomplex getrennt. Diese Anlage sollte verdeutlichen, daß die Natur hier dem Vergnügen und der Muse diente, im Gegensatz zur nutzbar gemachten Natur der Kulturlandschaft im Belice-Tal. Solche Gärten sind im sizilianischen Hinterland stets von einer Mauer oder einer dichten Baumreihe umrahmt. Mehr oder weniger nah am Haus gelegen, setzen sie Zeichen inmitten der sonnendurchglühten Landschaft: Hier befindet sich ein Haus, Wasser, der Mensch.

Der Garten der Case Di Stefano liegt am Fuße des Abhangs, war einmal von Mauern umfaßt und von sich kreuzenden Wegen strukturiert. Buchsbaumhecken markierten die Wege. Sie liefen auf einen zentralen Punkt zu – den Platz mit der Statue eines Ahnen. Dort, wo der Garten mit dem Hügel verschmolz, war eine erhöhte Promenade angelegt worden, gesäumt von einer Doppelreihe Washingtonia-Palmen, mit Wasserbecken und kleinen Bänken. Von der Promenade gelangte man auf einen Weg, der zum höchsten Punkt des Gartens führte – hier befand sich ein Wachtturm.

Unsere erste Arbeit bestand darin, einen Entwurf auszuarbeiten für die Renovierung und Umnutzung der Gebäude. Wichtig war dabei die Anordnung der Räume auf verschiedenen Niveaus – dieser Niveauplan stellte die Grundlage unserer Arbeit dar. Durch Weglassen, Durchschneiden und Rekonstruieren von Gebäudeteilen und Freiräumen wollten wir den ehemals geschlossenen, privaten Komplex so weit öffnen, daß er seiner zukünftigen Nutzung als öffentliches Kulturzentrum gerecht würde. Um den »baglio« ordnen sich die Gebäude nun freier an; jedes ist in Funktion und Form klar definiert. Um die Einzelbauten der Case Di Stefano miteinander zu verbinden, haben wir ein neues System von Wegen, Höfen, Durchgangsterrassen, Patios und Passagen geschaffen. Die umgebende Landschaft ist Teil

intended to serve a pleasurable purpose in contrast to the more utilitarian ones of the rest of the land. In the Sicilian hinterland such gardens were always surrounded by a wall or a row of closely-planted trees. Located close to the house, they indicated to the traveller approaching them through the sun-drenched landscape that here was a place where one would find a house, water, people. At Case Di Stefano, the ornamental garden still lies at the foot of the slope, surrounded by walls and divided up by boxwood paths that run to a central statue of a manorial ancestor. A raised promenade with a double row of *Washingtonia* palms, basins and benches runs along the upper end of the garden, where it merges in with the slope, and from here a path leads up to a watchtower at the garden's highest point.

Our first task consisted of drawing up a design for the renovation of the old buildings in keeping with their new purpose. The way they were situated on various levels formed the basis of our work. Our intention was to open up the formerly private, closed-in complex, as befitting

Case Di Stefano, Gibellina, Sicily
Client: Municipality of Gibellina Nuova
Architects: Marcella Aprile, Roberto Collovà, Teresa La Rocca
Planning: 1982–1996
Construction: 1984–1996
Size: 2,980 square metres (roofed area), 4,830 square metres (outdoor spaces), 2,420 square metres (garden)
Costs: LIT 8,500 million

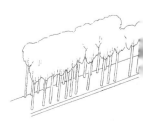

a public culture centre, by eliminating parts of some buildings and dissecting and reconstructing others. We arranged the ones we kept in a freer manner around the *baglio,* and clearly defined each as to form and function. We then created a new system of pathways, stepways, courts, passages and patios to join them together. The surrounding landscape was made part of this system in that we opened up the two main courts on one side, and provided the high walls that form the edges of the terraced stepways with slits and openings to "let in" the countryside.

The interior pathways and passages are a continuation of those on the outside. Originally, the lower floor of the manor house consisted of a row of storage rooms only accessible from the outside. These we now provided with new access in the form of a gallery, and applied the same principle upstairs to link the sleeping quarters on the first floor. Here a gallery passes through a tower at one end of the building and opens up onto a narrow outdoor passage that provides access to the upper court and the palm promenade further up.

We completely reconstructed the old buildings that enclose the upper court, and created a new road between the old and new parts of the centre. This road organises the buildings and open spaces according to a new hierarchy and lends them an urban touch, thus increasing the public character of the whole complex.

dieses Systems, denn beide Höfe sind zu ihr geöffnet. Durch Fensteröffnungen und Spalten in den hohen Umfassungsmauern der Terrassen dringt die Landschaft zudem in diese »Innenräume« ein.

Im Inneren der Gebäude verlängern sich die Wege und Passagen des Außenraumes: Das herrschaftliche Haus besaß im Erdgeschoß ursprünglich aneinandergereihte, nur von außen zugängliche Lagerräume – diese erhalten nun einen neuen Zugang über eine lange Galerie im Inneren. Entsprechend haben wir den Herbergstrakt im Obergeschoß erschlossen: Ein Galeriegang verbindet die Wohnräume miteinander und führt am einen Ende des Gebäudes über einen Turm auf einen seitlichen Durchgang, am anderen auf den oberen Hof und von dort auf die Palmen-Promenade.

Im Norden rekonstruierten wir die alten Gebäude vollständig. Zum Hof hin schufen wir eine neue Durchgangsstraße – als virtuelle Trennlinie verläuft sie zwischen den neuen und den wiederaufgebauten Teilen des Landguts, ordnet Bauten und Freiräume in einer neuen Hierarchie, verleiht ihnen etwas Städtisches und verstärkt so den öffentlichen Charakter der gesamten Anlage.

Axonometrie und Wegeplan der Case Di Stefano: 1 alte Zufahrt, 2 Erschließungsweg, 3 unterer Hof, 4 oberer Hof, 5 Werkstätten, 6 Herberge und Arbeitsräume, 7 Museum für Großplastiken, 8 Büros, 9 Wechselausstellungen, 10 Lager, Garage, Hausmeister, 11 Olivenhain, 12 Palmenweg zum alten Garten.
Case Di Stefano: Axonometric projection and path system. 1 Old drive, 2 Access path, 3 Lower court, 4 Upper court, 5 Workshops, 6 Hostel and workrooms, 7 Sculpture museum, 8 Offices, 9 Exhibitions, 10 Storerooms, garage and janitor, 11 Olive grove, 12 Palm-flanked pathway to the old garden.

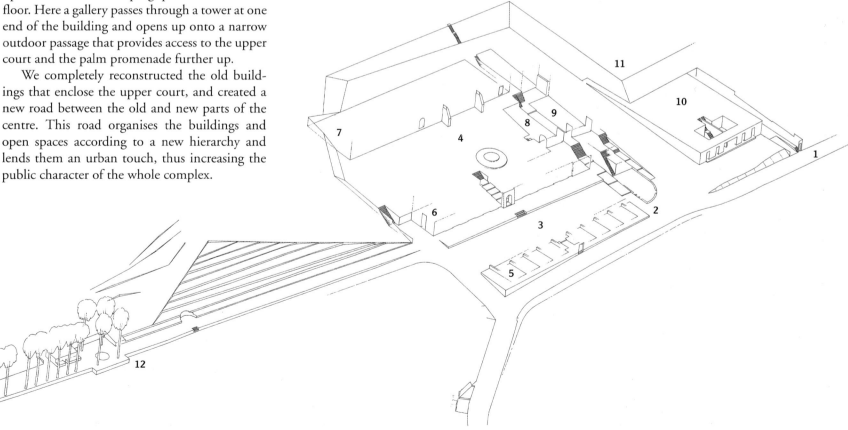

Schouwburgplein: Mehr Bild als Platz ?

Schouwburgplein: more of an image than a square ?

The globalisation of economics is forcing many big European cities to restructure. The townscape plays an important role in the process, for both the media and investors propagate a city's aesthetic quality. After all, the triumph of television has made our appetites for images grow enormously. Anything that cannot be made into an effective picture does not have a chance on the international market. New technologies have reinforced this trend even more. Many municipalities present themselves in the Internet. It's the done thing to stand out in the dance of competing cities in the net of nets. Besides the hard facts, anyone making a virtual visit to a city expects to find beautiful pictures on their screen.

In Rotterdam the municipal council foresaw these developments and prescribed a major facelift for the city. One renewal site was the Rotterdam harbour. Its restructuring has secured its position as a pillar of Dutch economics. In parallel, a new open space policy was developed that has endowed many places in town with a lot of character. With new urban open spaces as its trademark, Rotterdam has now moved ahead quite a bit in the Monopoly game of the metropolises.

One of Rotterdam's top prestigious projects was the Schouwburgplein (see *Topos* 20). Only a few steps away from the railway station, the square used to be a sorry sight: derelict, empty, disgusting. Renewal was overdue and was commissioned from the landscape architect Adriaan Geuze. He wanted to make the square into a place "where all kinds of people meet: the customers of the surrounding shops, the employees of the nearby offices, young people, children, the residents of the district and the people going to the movies." In other words, it was to be a public

Sophie Rousseau

Die Globalisierung der Wirtschaft zwingt viele europäische Großstädte zur Umstrukturierung. Dabei spielt das Stadtbild eine entscheidende Rolle, denn Medien wie Investoren propagieren die ästhetische Qualität einer Stadt. Schließlich ist mit dem Siegeszug des Fernsehens unser Appetit auf Bilder enorm gewachsen – und was sich nicht ansprechend ins Bild bringen lässt, hat auf dem internationalen Markt keine Chance. Die neuen Technologien haben diesen Trend noch verstärkt. Viele Kommunen präsentieren sich heute im Internet – es gehört dazu, im Reigen der konkurrierenden Städte im Netz der Netze präsent zu sein. Doch wer auch immer einer Stadt einen virtuellen Besuch abstattet, verlangt auf seinem Bildschirm neben harten Fakten selbstredend auch schöne Bilder.

In Rotterdam hat der Stadtrat diese Entwicklung vorausgesehen und seiner Stadt ein umfangreiches Lifting verordnet. Es betrifft zum einen den Rotterdamer Hafen – die Neustrukturierung sichert seine Position als Pfeiler der niederländischen Wirtschaft. Parallel dazu wurde eine Freiraumpolitik entwickelt, die der Stadt an vielen Orten ein charaktervolles Gesicht beschert hat. Mit den neuen städtischen Freiräumen als Markenzeichen ist Rotterdam um einiges nach vorne gerückt im Monopoly der Metropolen.

Der Vorzeigeplatz Rotterdams illustriert, wie ein städtischer Freiraum zum physisch wie virtuell erlebbaren öffentlichen Ort wird.

Rotterdam's showpiece square illustrates how a urban open space can turn into a public space that is experienced both physically and virtually.

Rotterdam Schouwburgplein
1990 und jetzt: Für den einst
verwahrlosten Platz entwarf
der Landschaftsarchitekt
Adriaan Geuze eine Bühne, auf
der sich alle möglichen Leute
treffen sollen. Vor dem Hintergrund der Rotterdamer Skyline
soll der Platz Podium sein für
vielfältige Aktivitäten.

Rotterdam's Schouwburgplein
in 1990 and today: for the formerly derelict square the landscape architect Adriaan Geuze
designed a stage on which all
kinds of people could meet.
With the Rotterdam skyline in
the background the square was
to provide a podium for a variety of activities.

Zu Rotterdams Prestige-Projekten ersten Ranges zählt der Schouwburgplein (siehe Topos 20). Nur ein paar Schritte vom Bahnhof entfernt, bot der Platz einst einen traurigen Anblick: verwahrlost, leer, abstoßend. Eine Neugestaltung stand an und wurde dem Landschaftsarchitekten Adriaan Geuze übertragen. Er wollte aus dem Platz einen Ort machen, »an dem sich alle möglichen Leute treffen: die Kundschaft der umliegenden Geschäfte, die Angestellten der nahen Büros, Jugendliche, Kinder, Einwohner des Viertels und Kinobesucher« – einen öffentlichen Raum ganz im klassischen Sinne des Wortes also. Doch fragt es sich, wie wir wohl in Zukunft mit dieser Art öffentlicher Räume umgehen werden?

Ohne dass es uns groß beunruhigt, haben sich die neuen Technologien in unser tägliches Leben eingeschlichen. Wir schreiben uns nicht mehr, sondern schicken uns e-mails. Wir stehen nicht mehr Schlange vor dem Bankschalter, sondern überweisen Geld via Telebanking, bequem vom Heim-Computer aus. Kaum jemand braucht noch aufs Rathaus zu gehen, um ein Formular zu holen, Amtsgeschäfte lassen sich in vielen Gemeinden bereits über eine kommunale Homepage abwickeln. Die Welt kommt täglich mit mehr Angeboten via Internet nach Hause, niemand muss sie mehr draußen suchen. Selbst Einkäufe werden zunehmend im Netz erledigt, wie

space in the classic sense of the word. The question is how are we going to deal with this kind of public space in the future?

Without worrying us much, new technologies have crept into our daily life. We don't write to each other any more, we send e-mails. We don't queue in front of a bank teller any more but zap money around with ease by tele-banking from a personal computer at home. Hardly anyone needs to go to city hall any more to pick up a form; in many municipalities official business can be taken care of on the city's homepage. The world comes into our homes with more offers every day via Internet, we don't have to look for them outside any more. Even shopping is done on the net more and more often, as the explosive rise of e-commerce proves. Anyone thinking that our need for sensual experiences, such as smells, sets limits to the net is underestimating the inventiveness of the engi-

Zwischen Lüftungstürmen und Lichtmasten plazierten die Planer lange Holzbänke, wo sich Passanten niederlassen und das Geschehen vom Rand des Platzes aus beobachten sollen.

Between ventilation towers and light masts, the long wooden benches were placed where passers-by could sit and watch the goings-on from the edge of the square.

neers. For we will soon be able to buy programmes along the lines of colour printers that perfume our rooms to suit our taste.

Technical innovations have always awakened as many fears as enthusiasms. Thus some critics now think that the increasingly popular new technologies will endanger the future of traditional public space. They think it is becoming useless because contacts among people are taking place elsewhere. Certainly the new media do play an important role and are moving the customary forms of encounter in the city's public space, on the streets, boulevards and squares, into the background. Perhaps in the not too distant future we will meet while surfing in the Internet instead of face to face on the terrace of a café, even an Internet café.

In this context the Schouwburgplein could be called an extraordinarily avant-garde place. It is not especially suited for direct physical encounters between people. It is much rather a place of emptiness, of beautiful emptiness, of movement in empty space. People do not meet here; they run past each other, across the square or along it. Of course organised events with big audiences do take place on the square, but the Rotterdamers seldom congregate here spontaneously. Its furnishings do not exactly invite people to linger. The raised podium above pathway level serves people as an improvised bench at the edge much more often than as a stage for spontaneous performances in the centre. Should there be a performance, people could not even enjoy it from the terraces of the cafés, for these are on the other side of the pedestrian zone, at some distance and clearly lower than the main part of the square. The view from the cafés extends only to the back of the long bench that borders the square and to the

der explosionsartige Anstieg des e-commerce beweist. Wer glaubte, dass unser Bedürfnis nach sinnlichen Erlebnissen, etwa Gerüchen, dem Netz Grenzen setzen würde, hat die Erfindungsgabe der Ingenieure unterschätzt. Denn bald werden wir uns Programme kaufen können, die nach dem Prinzip eines Farbdruckers unsere Räume nach Gusto parfümieren.

Technische Neuerungen haben zu jeder Zeit ebenso Ängste geweckt wie Begeisterung hervorgerufen. So meint heute manch kritischer Kopf, dass die immer populärer werdenden neuen Technologien die Zukunft des traditionellen öffentlichen Raumes gefährden: Er würde zunehmend nutzlos, Kontakte von Mensch zu Mensch würden woanders stattfinden. Sicher spielen die neuen Medien dabei eine wichtige Rolle und rücken die althergebrachten Formen der Begegnung in den Hintergrund, in den öffentlichen Räumen der Stadt, auf den Straßen, Boulevards und Plätzen. Vielleicht treffen wir uns in nicht allzu ferner Zukunft eher beim Surfen im Internet als direkt auf der Terrasse eines Cafés, und sei es auch ein Internet-Café.

Vor diesem Hintergrund lässt sich der Schouwburgplein als ein außerordentlich avantgardistischer Ort bezeichnen. Er eignet sich nicht besonders für die direkte, physische Begegnung von Menschen. Er ist viel eher ein Ort der Leere, der schönen Leere, der Bewegung im Leeren. Hier trifft man sich nicht, hier läuft man aneinander vorbei, über den Platz hinweg oder an ihm entlang. Natürlich finden hier organisierte Veranstaltungen mit großem Publikum statt, aber spontan versammeln sich die Rotterdamer selten auf dem Platz. So wie er ausgestattet ist, lädt er nicht gerade zum Verweilen ein. Sein über Fußwegniveau erhobenes Podium dient den Menschen am Rand viel öfter als improvisierte Bank denn als Bühne für spontane Inszenierungen in der Mitte. Gäbe es solche, könnte man sie von den Caféterrassen auch gar nicht genießen, denn jene liegen auf der anderen Seite der Fußgängerachse, auf Abstand und deutlich niedriger als die Hauptfläche des Platzes. Von den Cafés aus fällt der Blick lediglich auf die Rückseite der langen Bank, die den Platz begrenzt, und auf die technischen Einrichtungen am Rande des Podiums. Und auch das Mega-Kino gegenüber bietet keine Logenplätze – das Foyer hat eine geschlossene Fassade.

Hingegen eröffnet der Schouwburgplein den Bildhungrigen aus den Marketingabteilungen privater wie öffentlicher Unternehmen vielfältige Möglichkeiten. Seine Ästhetik verführt Werbefachleute und Webdesigner. Die Rotterdam City Development Corporation lädt zum Beispiel auf ihrer Homepage zu einem virtuellen Spaziergang durch die Stadt – natürlich

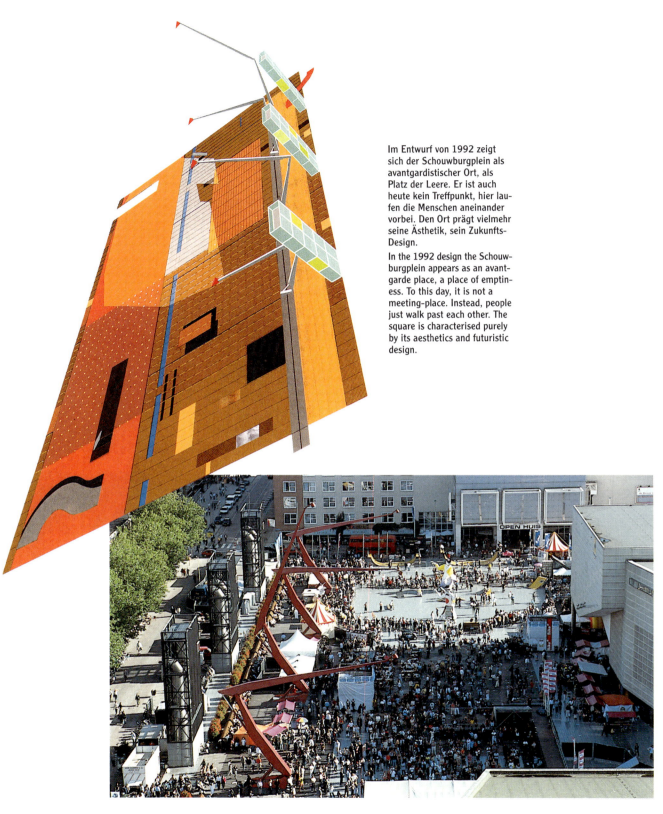

Im Entwurf von 1992 zeigt sich der Schouwburgplein als avantgardistischer Ort, als Platz der Leere. Er ist auch heute kein Treffpunkt, hier laufen die Menschen aneinander vorbei. Den Ort prägt vielmehr seine Ästhetik, sein Zukunfts-Design.

In the 1992 design the Schouwburgplein appears as an avantgarde place, a place of emptiness. To this day, it is not a meeting-place. Instead, people just walk past each other. The square is characterised purely by its aesthetics and futuristic design.

Nur bei organisierten Veranstaltungen versammeln sich auf dem Platz zahlreiche Menschen. Die Rotterdamer zwingt sonst nichts hierher.

People gather on the square only for organised events. Nothing else attracts the Rotterdamers to this place.

Um das perfekte Bild des Platzes – und damit auch seine Marketingwirkung – dauerhaft zu erhalten, wird die Stadt viel Geld für seine Pflege aufwenden müssen. Ist der Lack einmal ab, wird sich wohl niemand mehr für den Schouwburgplein interessieren.

In order to maintain the perfect image of the square – and thus its marketability – over the long term, the city will have to invest a lot of money in its maintenance. Once the veneer is scratched, it is unlikely that anyone will be interested in the Schouwburgplein.

Das über Fußgängerniveau gehobene Podium dient den Menschen eher als Sitzgelegenheit denn als Bühne – die Erwartungen der Planer haben sich nicht erfüllt.

The raised podium above pedestrian level serves more as a seat than a stage – the planners' expectations were not fulfilled.

über den Schouwburgplein (www.city.rotterdam.nl). Die Homepage der Kulturhauptstadt Rotterdam 2001, genannt »Rotterdam Experience 2001«, unterstreicht ihren Slogan »Just different« mit einem Foto der beweglichen Leuchten des Platzes. Das Zukunfts-Design hat auch den Leiter des europäischen Progress Software Technical Support Center auf die Idee gebracht, sein Interview mit einem Foto zu schmücken, das ihn vor der Kulisse des Platzes zeigt.

Wenn der Schouwburgplein durch seine Ästhetik überzeugt, dann ist sie zugleich auch seine Achillesferse. Denn die Pflege dieses Freiraums duldet nicht die geringste Nachlässigkeit. Im Null Komma nichts wäre sonst der Lack ab vom strahlenden Markenzeichen. Ikonen müssen perfekt sein, wie Mannequins, die weder das Recht noch die Zeit zum Altern haben. Sie sind oft schon »out«, bevor sie wirklich alt sind. Die Welt der Bilder ist grausam. Aus diesem Grunde wird der Unterhalt des Schouwburgplein auf kurze oder lange Sicht viel Geld kosten. Seine Materialien und ihre Verarbeitung sind zu fein für die Nutzung, der sie standhalten müssen. Man mag sich damit trösten, dass der öffentliche Raum sich im schlechtesten wie im besten Sinne in die virtuellen Welten hinein verlagern wird. Die Pflege des Bildes, der virtuellen Schönheit, kostet zwar nichts – aber ein Bild kann eben schnell veralten. Dann wird der Platz auf seine physische Wirklichkeit zurückgeworfen, und man darf sich wohl die Frage stellen, was aus dem Pionierbauwerk wird, das eine neue Zeit eingeläutet hat, wenn seine Sternstunde vorüber ist?

technical facilities on the edge of the podium. The mega-cinema opposite does not provide any box seats either; its foyer has a closed facade.

On the other hand, the Schouwburgplein provides plenty of opportunities for the picture-hungry staff of the marketing departments of private and public enterprises. Its aesthetics seduce advertising experts and website designers. On its homepage the Rotterdam City Development Corporation, for instance, invites us to take a virtual walk through the city – and of course across the Schouwburgplein ((www.city.rotterdam.nl)). The homepage of the Culture Capital Rotterdam 2001, called Rotterdam Experience 2001 underscores its slogan "Just different" with a photo of the movable lamps on the square.

While the Schouwburgplein's aesthetics are convincing, they are also its Achilles heel. For the maintenance of this open space will not stand the slightest negligence. The veneer would come off the city's gleaming trademark in no time at all. Icons have to be perfect, like models, who have neither the right nor the time to age. They are often 'out' even before they are really old. The world of images is cruel. This is why the maintenance of the Schouwburgplein will cost a lot of money in the short and the long run. Its materials and installations are too high-grade for the use they have to stand up to. One can console oneself that public space will be shifting in the worst and the best sense to virtual realms. While the maintenance of the image, of virtual beauty, costs nothing, a picture can quickly become dated. The square will then be cast back upon its physical reality. We may well ask what will become of the pioneering structure that has rung in a new era once its historic moment is over.

Die Via Mazzini in Verona

Via Mazzini in Verona

Boris Podrecca

Via Mazzini is the lifeline of Verona. For the Veronese this street is on the one hand the carrier of the city's memory, evidence to the resistance to urban morphological change of any kind throughout history. On the other it is the city's most lively and vital umbilical cord, linking Verona's sitting room, the Arena and Piazza Bra, with its kitchen, Piazza delle Erbe.

The street originated in the Roman *decumanum*, the north-south main axis of the Roman camp. The official strictness of the Roman grid was distorted and softened in the course of

Die Via Mazzini ist die Lebensader der Stadt. Für die Veroneser ist sie einerseits die Erinnerungsachse, ein Zeugnis des Widerstandes gegenüber allen stadtmorphologischen Veränderungen im Laufe der Geschichte, und andererseits die wichtigste Nabelschnur, welche den Salon der Stadt, die Arena und die Piazza Bra, mit der Küche Veronas, der Piazza delle Erbe, verbindet.

Der Straßenzug hat seinen Ursprung in der wichtigen Achse des römischen Dekumanum, der Süd-Nord verlaufenden römischen Lagerstraße. Die institutionelle Strenge des römischen Rasters wurde im Laufe der Zeit entstellt und ver-

Geschichte und profane Notwendigkeiten formen den neuen Rahmen für das geschäftige Stadtleben im Herzen von Verona.

History and everyday needs determine a new framework for the busy urban life of residents and visitors in the heart of Verona.

Via Mazzini, Verona
Client: City of Verona, Roads and Urban Furniture Department
Architects: Boris Podrecca and Domenico La Marca
Co-worker: Alberto dalla Torre
Total area: 4,100 square metres
Costs: ITL 1,500,000,000.
Realisation: 1995 – 1998

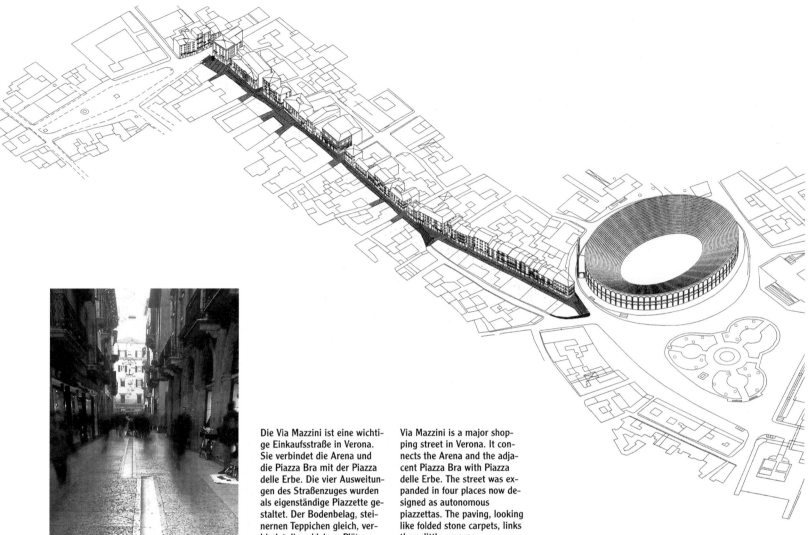

Die Via Mazzini ist eine wichtige Einkaufsstraße in Verona. Sie verbindet die Arena und die Piazza Bra mit der Piazza delle Erbe. Die vier Ausweitungen des Straßenzuges wurden als eigenständige Piazzette gestaltet. Der Bodenbelag, steinernen Teppichen gleich, verbindet diese kleinen Plätze.

Via Mazzini is a major shopping street in Verona. It connects the Arena and the adjacent Piazza Bra with Piazza delle Erbe. The street was expanded in four places now designed as autonomous piazzettas. The paving, looking like folded stone carpets, links these little squares.

Die in der Mitte liegenden Canaletti leiten das Wasser ab nach den für Verona typischen kurzen aber heftigen Regengüssen. Die steinernen Abflüsse betonen die Achse der Via Mazzini.

'Canaletti' down the middle of the street allow rainwater to drain off after the short but heavy rains typical for Verona. The stone drains emphasise the axis of Via Mazzini.

time. Later needs of the city widened the street with expansions in four places, creating four amorphous areas.

Via Mazzini itself represents a dichotomy between the street above ground with its organic irregular movement and the well-preserved underground grid of the camp with remains of the Roman forum, cemeteries and basilicas.

This dualism was partly utilised as a leitmotiv for the new design of Via Mazzini. On the one hand there are real and legible carriers of information on the history of the city, such as bronze reliefs set in stone tiles. On the other hand important underground traces show up in the paving materials as an abstract picture independent of the overall concept. The expansions interrupting the continuity of the street's line were not reversed back to their original state. On the contrary, they were further alienated from the street to form autonomous and independent small piazzas (piazzettas). Nevertheless, these public spaces evoke memory images among the people of Verona and bring particular places of the past to mind.

The first expansion, a square forming a foyer next to the Arena, symbolises the Roman element of the city in its texture. Further along, in the area still called 'alle campane' (by the bells) by the Veronese today, is the site of the former municipal foundry, only part of which is preserved. An echo of this memory is given material form in a central, concave, bronze fountain – the opposite of a convex segment of a real bell. The direction in which all the streets run that lead up to it is emphasised either by paving materials or the perspective. In contrast to the dynamics of the first two, the third widening introduces a tranquil

weichlicht. Die späteren Bedürfnisse der Stadt haben vier Ausweitungen in die Straße hineingerissen. Die eigentliche Via Mazzini bildet eine Dichotomie: die oberirdische Straße mit ihrer organhaften, gebrochenen Bewegung und die unterirdische, noch ziemlich gut erhaltene Rasterstadt mit Überresten des Forum Romanums, der Friedhöfe und der Basiliken. Dieser Dualismus wird teilweise auch als Leitmotiv des neuen Entwurfes benützt. Einerseits gibt es Informationsträger der Stadtgeschichte wie bronzene Reliefs, die in die Steinplatten eingelassen sind. Andererseits erscheinen un-

point in Via Mazzini. Traced onto the ground are the contours of the former ghetto, demolished to make room for a monumental building dating from the late Fascist period. A monolithic bench and a calligraphic inscription in bronze running

terirdische Spuren im Pflasterbelag als ein von der Gesamtkonzeption unabhängiges, abstraktes Bild. Die den Straßenzug störenden Ausweitungen werden nicht auf ihren Entwicklungsursprung zurückkorrigiert. Ganz im Gegenteil: Sie werden in Richtung unabhängiger Piazzette verfremdet. Trotzdem evozieren diese kleinen öffentlichen Räume Erinnerungsbilder.

parallel to it provide a memorial and encourage reflection about the past in the midst of the busy traffic in this spot.

The last piazzetta opens onto Verona's market square, Piazza delle Erbe. The textures on the ground underscore the progression. A kiosk indicates the spatial interface and refers to the commercial character of the location.

Die erste Ausweitung – ein an der Arena gelegener Foyer-Platz – versinnbildlicht in seinem texturalen Aufbau das Römische der Stadt. In der weiteren Folge, im noch heute von den Veronesern »alle campane« genannten Bereich, gab es eine, jetzt nur noch partiell vorhandene, große Stadtgießerei. Das Echo dieser Erinnerung wird durch einen zentrischen, konkaven, bronzenen Brunnen materialisiert – im Gegensatz zum reellen, konvexen Glockensegment. Die Richtungen sämtlicher hierher führender Straßen werden entweder in der Textur der Oberflächen oder perspekti-

Poller und Brunnen sind aus Bronze gefertigt. Material und Form des Brunnens auf der zweiten Piazzetta stellen historische Bezüge zu einer ehemaligen großen Gießerei her. Auch der Name des Stadtteils "alle campane" erinnert an die dort gegossenen Glocken.

The bollards and fountain are made of bronze. The material and form of the fountain in the second piazzetta is an historical reference to the big former municipal foundry. The name of this district, 'alle campane' also recalls the bells once cast here.

Bronzereliefs sind in die Steinplatten eingelassen und infor-
mieren die Passanten über die
Stadtgeschichte. Zu sehen sind
das strenge Raster der römischen Stadt sowie der heutige
Stadtgrundriss.

Bronze reliefs embedded in the
flagstones inform passers-by
about urban history. The relief
shows the underlying strict grid
of the Roman camp with today's street plan oriented on it
despite organic distortions.

These four different small squares are interlinked by a series of 'folded stone carpets' on the ground. The width of these carpets is based on the average width of the eaves overhang on Veronese houses. Thus the texture of this central paving strip contributes to the sense of space along the street. Folded over, the strip also doubles the stone inlets in the ground. This measure is designed for rapid rainwater drainage, especially in view of Verona's short but heavy downpours. It also explains the form of the 'canaletti', which look like zippers running down the middle of the street. These little channels emphasise and lend rhythm to the main axis of Via Mazzini visually.

The stone for the 'carpets' was quarried in nearby Prun. The individual tiles of the Rosso Verona and Rosso Assiago that lend the street a polychrome character can be cut to a size of up to 2 x 1.5 metres and are 20 centimetres thick. Thus the texture of the ground should be understood more as a powerful monolithic structure than a layer or skin. It forms a kind of floor for the level of the worldly street and ceiling for that of the underground archaeological town.

Nevertheless, all these considerations and configurations are perceived by the average passer-by to only a limited extent. As Via Mazzini is the actual shopping centre of Verona and a channel for the crowds of tourists and local residents, intellectualising metaphors were not applied to its design. It has no particular overall style. It consists of spaces whose new appearance developed from both earlier carriers of identity and unsentimental changes required for today's needs. They simply frame the comings and goings of everyday life in discreet fashion. Instead of a picture they form the mount.

visch betont. Die dritte Platzausweitung bietet im Gegensatz zur vorhergehenden Dynamik einen meditativen Ruhepol der Via Mazzini. Im Boden wird die ehemalige Kontur des durch einen Monumentalbau aus der spätfaschistischen Zeit zerstörten Ghettos nachgezeichnet. Eine monolithische Sitzbank und die parallel dazu verlaufende, kalligraphische bronzene Inschrift tragen gerade an diesem dichten Durchzugsgebiet zu Mahnung und Reflexion bei. Die letzte Piazzetta öffnet sich zum Veroneser Markt hin, der Piazza delle Erbe. Die Textur im Bodenaufbau unterstreicht diese Richtung und ein Verkaufskiosk, als räumliches Gelenk, weist auf den merkantilen Charakter des Ortes hin.

Diese vier verschiedenen kleinen Plätze werden mit steinernen Teppichen, die nacheinander gefaltet werden, verbunden. Ihr Breitenmaß entsteht aus der Analogie mit der durchschnittlichen Auskragung der Dachvorsprünge der Veroneser Häuser. Dadurch trägt die Textur dieses Mittelstreifens auch zum Raumgefüge des Straßenzuges bei. Ihre Faltung bewirkt auch eine Verdoppelung der steinernen Bodeneinläufe. Dies ist eine Maßnahme, die für das schnelle Abfließen des Wassers gedacht ist, vor allem in Hinblick auf die kurzen, aber heftigen Regengüsse Veronas. Demzufolge werden auch die fast einem Reißverschluss gleichenden und mittig liegenden Canaletti ausgebildet – sie betonen und rhythmisieren die optische Führungsachse der Via Mazzini. Die steinernen Teppiche stammen aus den benachbarten Veroneser Prun-Steinbrüchen. Der Rosso Verona und der Rosso Assiago geben der Straße einen polychromen Charakter. Die einzelnen Platten können bis zu einem Maß von 2 x 1,50 Metern zugeschnitten werden und haben eine Stärke von etwa 20 Zentimeter. Dadurch ist die Bodentextur eher als ein starkes, monolithisches Konstrukt denn als Steinhaut zu verstehen. Sie bildet eine Art Geschossdecke zwischen dem profanen Straßenzug und der unterirdischen, archäologischen Stadt.

Doch alle diese Überlegungen beziehungsweise Konfigurationen sind für den durchschnittlichen Passanten nur beschränkt wahrnehmbar. Da die Via Mazzini das eigentliche Einkaufszentrum Veronas ist und einen Kanal für das Gedränge von Touristen und Einheimischen darstellt, sind hier keine intellektualisierenden Metaphern angewandt worden. Es sind Räume, deren neues Erscheinungsbild sowohl aus früheren Identitätsträgern als auch durch unsentimentale, für die Ist-Zeit notwendige Veränderungen entstanden ist. Sie rahmen lediglich diskret das Kommen und Gehen des Lebens. Sie sind weniger Bild, sondern vielmehr Passepartout.

Der Ingólfstorg in Reykjavik

Ingólfstorg, Reykjavik

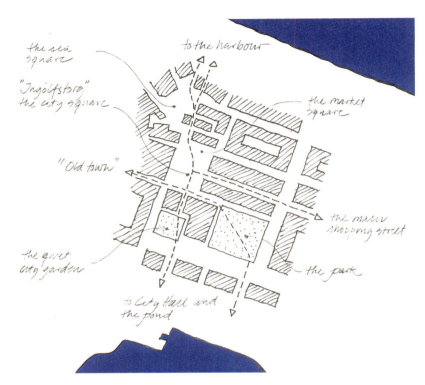

Helga Benediktsdóttir

Zwei zusammenhängende Stadtplätze bilden die neue Mitte der isländischen Hauptstadt Reykjavik. Rechtzeitig zur 50-Jahr-Feier der Republik im Jahr 1994 wurde der Ingólfstorg fertig, der Grófartorg ist seit 1995 benutzbar. Beide Plätze gingen aus einem Wettbewerb hervor, zu dem sechs Architekturbüros eingeladen waren. Verkstaedi 3 gewann den ersten Preis für diese Umgestaltung eines ziemlich heruntergekommenen Innenstadtquartiers an einer belebten Straßenkreuzung.

Ein Platz inmitten der isländischen Hauptstadt erinnert an den Stadtgründer Ingólfur und bietet dessen Erben neuen Freiraum.

A square at the heart of the Icelandic capital looks back to the city founder Ingólfur and provides his descendants with new open space.

Wir versuchten, einen Stadtraum zu schaffen, der sich trotz aller modernen Anforderungen an die Geschichte anlehnt. Schon die Namensgebung hat ja eine große Bedeutung. Ingólfstorg ist nach dem Wikinger Ingólfur benannt, der sich im Jahre 874 in Island ansiedelte. Der Sage nach

In the March of 1992, the city council of Reykjavik invited six architects offices to take part in a closed competition for the renovation of a somewhat run-down area of downtown Reykjavik. Verkstaedi 3 won the first prize in the scheme, which includes the creation of a new public square.

The development was divided into two parts, the first of which, Ingólfstorg, was completed in 1994 in time for the 50th anniversary of the founding of the Icelandic republic.

Our major concern was to create an urban space that would address the physical and historic issues of the site and revitalize the area. This has been achieved by integrating public spaces and promenades into a network of spatial sequences and linking the lakeside City Hall to the harbour.

The fundamental principles of our design draw on the power of nature, history and technology and an understanding of the poetry of the place, which is named for Ingólfur, the Viking chieftain who settled the island in 874. As a well-known saga tells, "Ingólfur threw the columns of his throne into the sea, vowing he would settle wherever they drifted ashore. He arrived by sea at the place where his columns were washed up, and saw hot steam rising from the earth. He named the place Reykjavik (steam bay)."

In order to better cope with the height and small scale of the surrounding buildings, we divided the site into two zones: a large, rectangular area, the public square, and a frontal plaza for the Geysir community centre that can also be used as a market place.

Our proposal also included closing a gap in the southern wall of buildings to reinforce the

Tiefergelegt und von Mauern umschlossen bietet der Ingólfstorg in Reykjavik den auf Island so wichtigen Windschutz. Basalt und Granit sowie ein dreiteiliges Wasserensemble stehen für die urwüchsige Landschaft der Insel. Es entstand ein vielfältig nutzbarer Freiraum, der durch eine Säulenhalle mit Café in zwei Bereiche gegliedert wird.

Sunken and walled in, the Ingólfstorg in Reykjavik provides shelter from the wind, so important in Iceland. Basalt and granite as well as a tripartite water ensemble stand for the elemental landscape of the island. A free space for various uses evolved, divided into two areas by a columned hall with a café.

Der Ingólfstorg bildet den Mittelpunkt einer Sequenz von Räumen und Passagen, die die neue Stadthalle am See mit dem Hafen verbindet.

The Ingólfstorg forms the heart of a sequence of spaces and passages connecting the new city hall on the lake with the harbour.

warf er die Pfeiler seines Throns ins Meer und schwor, daß er sich dort niederlassen werde, wo das Holz an Land gespült wird. Dies geschah in einer Bucht, wo an Land heißer Dampf aus der Erde quoll. Hier landete er und nannte den Ort Reykjavik, was Rauchbucht heißt. Diese Poesie der isländischen Sagen wollten wir in den Plan übernehmen.

Gestalterisch bestand die Hauptaufgabe darin, eine Sequenz von Räumen und Passagen zu schaffen, die die neue Stadthalle am See mit dem Hafen verbindet. Durch die Randbebauung ergaben sich zwei Teilräume: ein weiter rechteckiger Bereich als öffentlicher Raum, sowie ein Platz vor dem Gemeindezentrum Geysir, der als Marktplatz dienen soll. Um den Raumeindruck zu verstärken, schlugen wir vor, im Süden eine Baulücke zu schließen. Da das Wetter in Island sehr stark den Alltag bestimmt, war es uns wichtig, den Wind abzuschirmen, um so die Nutzbarkeit des Platzes zu erhöhen. Dazu zogen wir an den beiden Längsseiten Mauern und legten den nach Norden ansteigenden Platz insgesamt tiefer. So erhielten wir einen geschützten Raum. Eine Säulenhalle trennt die beiden Platzbereiche, zugleich bietet sie Schutz und Platz für ein kleines Café. Vor den Kolonnaden befindet sich eine kleine Bühne für Veranstaltungen. Ein von Nord nach Süd verlaufendes rotes Granitband durchschneidet die Treppenstufen und bildet die Platzachse, die beide Bereiche verbindet und zudem drei interaktive Wasserelemente enthält. Der Brunnen symbolisiert den Regen, der fällt und unterirdisch abfließt. Das Wasser taucht in Kaskaden wieder auf und strömt über die Stufen. Es verschwindet schließlich als Dampf bei den Lavasteinen. Diese Säulen aus Lava stehen wiederum symbolisch für die Thronpfeiler des Ingólfur, der Dampf aus den Stahlrohren für Reykjavik und für die Technologie, die es den Isländern ermöglicht, überall im Land die geothermische Energie zu nutzen.

Selbstverständlich sollte für diesen repräsentativen Platz nur solides Material verwendet werden. Er wurde mit finnischem Granit belegt, die Mauern bestehen aus isländischem Basalt; die Säulenhalle wurde mit Granit verkleidet und trägt ein Kupferdach.

Architects: Verkstaedi 3:
Elín Kjartansdóttir, Haraldur Örn Jónsson, Helga Benediktsdóttir
Client: The City of Reykjavik
Site: Downtown Reykjavik, 4000 square metres
Construction period: 1993–1994
Cost: US-$ 2.7 millions

feeling of a coherent enclosure – in its physical as well as its metaphorical meaning.

The weather plays a dominant role on Iceland, and therefore providing shelter from the winds was the most important factor of our design concept as this will maximize daily recreational use. Accordingly we sunk the central area, which rises to the north, and erected stone walls to the sides to create a sheltered and attractive multipurpose outdoor space.

An open colonnade separates the two areas of the square while providing shelter and housing a small cafe that faces in both directions.

A stage for public meetings and other outdoor events has been integrated into the steps in front of the colonnade.

A broad band of red granite marked by three linked water elements runs along the north-south axis of the square, passing through the steps to connect the two zones. The first of the water elements is a little spring, then the water tumbles down the steps as a symbol of the country's various rivers and waterfalls, to disappear into the ground like the rain that falls and seeps away, to reappear in the form of steam at two lava columns further along.

The columns are naturally in reference to Ingólfur's throne, while the steam, which emerges from steel tubes, recalls the origin of the city's name and the use of natural hot water for heating purposes.

We placed great importance on the use of solid, good quality material and thus the square is laid out in Finnish granite, the walls are made of Icelandic greystone while the colonnade with the cafe itself is clad in granite and provided with a copper roof.

Der Gouvernementsplein in Bergen op Zoom

Gouvernementsplein in Bergen op Zoom

The town of Bergen op Zoom, which is located in the south-west of the Dutch province of Noord Brabant, flourished in the 16th century as a port located up-shore from Antwerp. Today it has a number of very old open spaces that are unique in terms of character, location and function. In 1999, an ambitious project was launched to upgrade the town's historic old quarter, which contains a number of these spaces. In the process, the Hilversum landscape architecture practice Karres en Brands was commissioned to come up with a design for Gouvernementsplein, one of the squares involved. This in turn initiated a process of reflection about open space design within the municipality and among project stakeholders.

Gouvernementsplein is one of the smaller squares in downtown Bergen op Zoom. Originally, it was part of a large infirmary that also included an orchard and a cemetery. The grounds were sold to the town council in 1668, and the infirmary building was made into a governor's residence. A new building, known as Governor's House, was erected in 1771, and at the time was the most important edifice in the locality. It later served as a military hospital and sappers' office, and it was not until the early 1920s that the square was formed.

Contribution to urban life. Before the upgrading project, the square was not particularly attractive, nor was it ever in much use. Thus one of the most important tasks facing our practice was to make it more popular. The first and perhaps most important step in the design process was our realisation that the success of a space is not solely dependent on the way it is equipped and designed. Rather, it has to be capable of adapting

Die Stadt Bergen op Zoom, gelegen im Südwesten der niederländischen Provinz Noord Brabant, erlangte im 16. Jahrhundert als Vorhafen von Antwerpen wirtschaftliche Blüte. Die Stadt verfügt heute über eine Reihe sehr alter öffentlicher Räume, die jeder für sich eine besondere Lage, einen eigenen Charakter und eine spezifische Funktion besitzen. Im Jahre 1999 rief die Gemeinde Bergen op Zoom ein ehrgeiziges Projekt ins Leben, das die historische Altstadt weiter aufwerten sollte. Mit der Vergabe des Gouvernementsplein an die Hilversumer Landschaftsarchitekten Karres und Brands begann für die Gemeinde und alle Beteiligten ein Reflektionsprozess über das Entwerfen im öffentlichen Raum.

Bart Brands
Karel Loeff

Der Gouvernementsplein ist einer der kleineren Plätze in der Innenstadt. Ursprünglich war er Teil eines großen Krankenhausgeländes, zu dem auch ein Obstgarten und ein Friedhof gehörten. Durch den Verkauf des Geländes an den Staatsrat im Jahre 1668 wurde aus dem Krankenhaus eine Gouverneursresidenz. Das Gouvernementshaus, das wichtigste Gebäude am Platz, entstand 1771 und sollte später als Militärhospital und Büro der Pioniere dienen. Erst zu Anfang der neunziger Jahre des 20. Jahrhunderts wurde auf dem Gelände ein Platz eingerichtet.

Ein Beitrag zum städtischen Leben. Der wenig attraktive Platz wurde bisher kaum angenommen. Eine der wichtigsten Aufgaben für unser Büro war es demnach, den Platz zu beleben. Der erste und vielleicht wichtigste Schritt im Entwurfs-

Der öffentliche Raum als Ökosystem: Gefragt ist kein statisches Korsett, sondern ein flexibles Konzept, das sich den Bedürfnissen anpasst.
Regarding public open space as a ecosystem has resulted in a flexible concept that can be adapted to the requirements of users.

to changing customs and wishes, and thus requires an equally dynamic design approach. Our solution regards public open space as a subtle but extremely vigorous ecosystem, whereby the term ecosystem does not refer to nature but to an abstract network of interacting components. In other words, the significance of an urban open space is largely determined by its relationship to other spaces and existing shops, and also by its location within the urban fabric, and the events that it attracts.

We thus realised that we not only had to analyse the wishes and requirements of the council, but that the square and the functions of the buildings surrounding it had to be taken into equal consideration. We accordingly drew up a study on the square's possible uses and functions and used it to initiate a discussion with the municipal planning group and responsible councillors. The goal of these discussions was to formulate a joint priority list as the basis for the actual design. One of the most important questions was whether the square was to retain its existing structure or return to earlier situations.

The design. The design that we drew up for Gouvernementsplein structures the square by means of one spatial measure, namely a fold in the ground. This intervention, which terminates at the southern end in a raised area, clearly assigns walking areas to the edges of the buildings. Parts of the space are marked with steel strips let into the ground to indicate the boundaries of street cafés. Public seating is also included, and two areas of lawn refer to the historical garden situation. A path runs between them like a carpet, leading to the main entrance of Governor's House and redirecting attention to the impor-

Wasserspiele beleben den Gouvernementsplatz in der Altstadt von Bergen op Zoom auf spielerische Art und Weise.
A playful element in the form of a water feature enlivens Gouvernementsplatz in the old quarter of Bergen op Zoom.

prozess war die Feststellung, dass Ausstattung und Gestaltung eines Ortes sich nur in begrenztem Maße auf den Erfolg des öffentlichen Raums auswirken. Die Möglichkeit, einen öffentlichen Raum für die sich verändernden Gewohnheiten und Wünsche flexibel zu halten, erfordert einen dynamischen Entwurfsansatz. Dabei kann der öffentliche Raum als subtiles, aber vor allem vitales Ökosystem aufgefasst werden. Dieses Ökosystem sehen wir nicht als Synonym für Natur, sondern für ein abstraktes Netzwerk von einander beeinflussenden und aufeinander reagierenden Komponenten. Die Bedeutung des öffentlichen Raums wird insbesondere von dem Verhältnis zu anderen Plätzen, den vorhandenen Geschäften, der Lage im Stadtraum und den dort möglichen Veranstaltungen bestimmt.

Anhand einer Studie konnte mit der Planungsgruppe der Gemeinde und den zuständigen Abgeordneten eine Diskussion über die möglichen Nutzungen und Funktionen des Platzes eingeleitet werden. Ziel war es, ein gemeinsames Prioritätenmodell zu erarbeiten, auf dessen Grundlage der eigentliche Entwurf entstehen konnte. Eine wichtige Frage war, ob der Platz seine bestehende städtebauliche Struktur beibehalten oder ob

Der Brunnen besteht aus mehreren Edelstahlplatten, auf die mit Lasertechnik Grundrisse der Stadt aufgebracht wurden (siehe Seite 105). Von Zeit zu Zeit emporschießende Fontänen machen den kleinen Platz zu einer Attraktion. Gut beobachten lässt sich das Spektakel von den Sitzstufen aus, die sich durch die Niveauunterschiede ergeben. Die Pflasterung des Platzes greift den Natursteinbelag im Stadtzentrum auf und wirkt zwischen den Rasenflächen wie ein Läufer. Eine Kombination aus geschliffenem portugiesischen und rauem schwedischen Granit ergänzt den italienischen Naturstein der Sitzstufe.

The fountain, which is let into the ground, consists of a number of stainless steel plates laser-etched with layouts of Bergen op Zoom (see page 105). Designed to make the small square a more popular place, the water feature and its occasional gushes of water can be watched from the seating step installed along the fold in the ground. The paving of the square refers to the natural stone surfacing in the downtown area, and takes on the effect of a strip carpet between the two areas of lawn. The combination of polished Portuguese granite setts and roughly-hewn Swedish granite forms a contrast to the Italian stone of the seating step.

auf frühere Situationen zurückgegriffen werden soll. Die Antwort: Es kommt neben der Analyse von Wünschen und Möglichkeiten seitens der Gemeinde vor allem darauf an, die Platzfläche und die umliegenden Funktionen gleichzeitig anzugehen.

Der Entwurf. Im ausgeführten Entwurf wird der Gouvernementsplein durch eine einzige räumliche Maßnahme strukturiert, nämlich durch das Falten der Grundfläche. Durch diesen Eingriff entsteht eine klare Wegeführung entlang der Fassaden. Der Knick im Platz endet an der Südseite mit einem Podium. Neben Sitzgelegenheiten gibt es auch Platz für Straßencafés, markiert mit Linien auf dem Boden. Zwei Rasenflächen, die auf die historische Gartensituation verweisen, lassen wieder eine direkte Orientierung auf den Haupteingang des Gouvernementgebäudes zu. Die Pflasterung zwischen den Rasenflächen wirkt wie ein Läufer.

Ein anderes Element im Entwurf ist der neue Brunnen an der Stelle der ehemaligen Kapelle. Aus kaum erhöhten, in den Boden eingelassenen Edelstahlplatten schießen Fontänen empor, um gleich darauf wieder zu verschwinden. In die Platten wurden mit Hilfe von Lasertechnik verschiedene Stadtgrundrisse von Bergen op Zoom geschnitten. Diese Spielerei hebt sich angenehm von der würdevollen Altstadt ab und scheint den Müßiggängern zuzuwinken. Sie illustriert die Vergänglichkeit und sorgt doch für eine längere Verweildauer der Besucher. Die Pflasterung des Platzes greift den Natursteinbelag auf, der bei der Sanierung des Zentrums verwendet wird. Eine Kombination aus geschliffenem portugiesischen Granitpflaster und rauem schwedischen Granit bildet die Basis des Belags. Am Knick entlang wird mit italienischen Natursteinbändern eine Sitzstufe ausgebildet, die gleichzeitig als Balancierstreifen dient und genug Platz für ein Podium lässt.

Entwurfsmethode. Die Tatsache, dass die Gemeinde den Platz in kürzester Zeit realisieren wollte, hat zu einer ungewöhnlichen Vorgehensweise geführt. Der Platz wurde ohne genau ausgearbeitete und detaillierte Entwurfszeichnungen ausgeführt. Im fortgeschrittenen Teil des Entwurfsprozesses wurden die Entwurfsvorschläge anhand zahlreicher Modelle, Skizzen und Prototypen diskutiert. So gab es Studien zur Überdeckelung des gesamten Platzes, zur Öffnung des Gouvernementgebäudes für die Öffentlichkeit, oder zur Errichtung eines Neubaus an der Stelle des ehemaligen Klosters. Anhand dieser Studien, die die politische Durchsetzbarkeit und das verfügbare Budget berücksichtigt, wurde das Bedarfsprogramm für den Platz formuliert. Dieses Programm wurde in eine abstrakte Skizze ohne De-

Gouvernementsplein, Bergen op Zoom,
The Netherlands
Client: Municipality of Bergen op Zoom
Landscape architects: Karres en Brands landschapsarchitecten – Bart Brands, Jim Navarro
Planning: 1998
Construction: 1999

tant building. At the former site of a chapel we also incorporated a fountain of stainless steel plates let into the ground, whereby the water shoots up through grids of various plans of Bergen op Zoom laser-etched into the steel. The playful element forms a pleasant contrast to the dignified character of the old quarter, and seems to attract people and hold their attention.

The paving of the square refers to the natural stone surfacing used for the renewal of the downtown area, and is based on a combination of polished Portuguese granite setts and roughly-hewn Swedish granite. A seating step made of strips of Italian stone is provided along the fold, and can be used as a defile for balancing. Room is also created in this way for an additional stage.

Design method. In the advanced stages of the design process, proposals were discussed on the basis of various mock-ups, sketches and prototypes, and it was considered whether to cover the whole square in concrete, and whether to open Governor's House to the public or erect a new building at the site of a former monastery. The studies involved were measured in terms of their political viability and available funding, and those finding favour were used as the basis for drawing up a requirements programme. The fact that the council wanted to execute the design as quickly as possible led to an unusual situation, in which the requirements programme was translated into a rough sketch showing the main direction of the design but not including any details or statement of materials. This vague study was used to start work on the actual execution. In other words, the square itself was a 1:1 mock-up, and as such was used as a real-life model for determining further steps.

By adopting this approach, the council took a risk that was highly unusual when it is considered that it had to accommodate a number of regulations and differing wishes. As for our design, it enables parts of the square to be changed at a later time, as in the case of the lawns, which may become a flowerbed or something else. This approach returns the historic square to its users and will enable them to adapt the subtle open space ecosystem to their needs whenever required.

taillierung und Materialbezeichnungen übersetzt, in der nur die Hauptlinien des Entwurfs festgelegt waren. Auf der Grundlage dieses Plans begann die Gemeinde mit der Ausführung. Der Platz wurde so gewissermaßen zum Modell im Maßstab 1:1, anhand dessen der definitive Entwurf weiter erarbeitet wurde. Die Gemeinde hat damit ein Risiko gewagt, das für einen Bauherren, der viele Wünsche, Richtlinien und Interessengruppen beachten muss, außergewöhnlich ist. Im Entwurf wurde berücksichtigt, dass Teile des Platzes sich im Laufe der Zeit verändern können. Der historische Platz wird damit den Nutzern zurückgegeben, die das subtile System öffentlicher Raum stets ihren Bedürfnissen anpassen können.

Bibliotheksplatz in Landskrona

Library precinct, Landskrona, Sweden

Monika Gora

Landskrona bedeutet Krone des Landes. Heute eine Kleinstadt, war Landskrona, am Öresund gelegen, einst von großer strategischer Bedeutung für Schweden. Die imposante Zitadelle wurde 1549 unter Christian III. errichtet. Nach der Zeit der massiven militärischen Befestigungen erlebte Landskrona im 18. Jahrhundert eine wirtschaftliche Blüte, die sich im Bau vieler Bürgerhäuser und öffentlicher Gebäude niederschlug. Diese Barockhäuser prägen noch heute das Stadtbild Landskronas. Eines dieser Gebäude ist das einstige Feuerwehrhaus, das heute die Bibliothek beherbergt. Der asphaltierte und eingezäunte Platz davor sollte mittels eines eingeladenen Wettbewerbs wieder zu dem werden, was er ursprünglich einmal war: ein städtischer Platz mit künstlerischem Anspruch, gestaltet als ein Ensemble skulpturaler Objekte.

Der Platz besteht aus einer einfachen Kiesfläche, an die sich ein Streifen aus Betonpflaster an der Gebäudekante anschließt; aus frei stehenden Bäumen und einer Buchenhecke, die spielerisch geschwungen den Eingangsbereich umfasst; aus einem Brunnen mit niedrigen, breiten, abgerundeten Kanten aus Beton, bei dem das Wasser aus mehreren Düsen strömt – auf die gleiche Art, wie wenn man einen Duschkopf in der Badewanne unter die Wasserfläche hält. Darüber hinaus finden sich drei sieben Meter hohe Kegel aus Metall, die in einer Linie aufgereiht auf dem Platz stehen und die schon von weitem zu sehen sind. Sie wirken durch das perforierte Metall wie Säulen aus Licht – tags wie nachts.

Der Brunnen rechts vor dem Eingang ist zu einem Treffpunkt der Jugendlichen geworden. Sie sitzen, liegen und spielen am Brunnenrand, und manchmal fällt auch einer ins Wasser. Der Platz erlaubt es, sich mit dem Rad oder zu Fuß frei zu bewegen.

Die Gestaltung ist äußerst schlicht, die Baukosten waren demgemäß niedrig. Trotzdem wird der Freiraum vor der Bibliothek sehr geschätzt und zählt mittlerweile zu den beliebtesten Stadtplätzen von Landskrona.

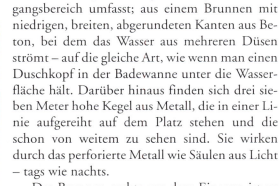

Kies, Kegel und Hecke: Der Bibliotheksvorplatz ist ein Ensemble skulpturaler Objekte, gestaltet nach künstlerischen Grundsätzen.

Gravel, cones and curved hedges: Reshaped according to artistic principles, the library precinct is now an ensemble of sculptural objects.

Landskrona means "crown of the country". The town, which is located on The Sound, was once of great strategic significance for Sweden, as proved by the imposing fortress erected during the reign of Christian III in 1549. After continued construction of military fortifications, Landskrona experienced a civilian heyday in the 18th century, when more residential houses began to be built, namely in a style that came to be known as Landskrona baroque. One of the edifices concerned was once the fire brigade building, and now houses the town library. A limited competition was held in 1997 to turn the fenced-in expanse of asphalt at its front into the kind of urban open space it originally was, complete with an ensemble of sculptural objects.

The winning entry by landscape architect Monika Gora has turned the zone into a simple area of gravel in which strips of concrete paving surround the building. The space now features solitary trees, curved beech hedges that playfully lead to the actual library entrance, and a fountain with low, wide concrete edges and water bubbling below the surface as if a shower head were being held in a bathtub of water. Also included is a row of three seven-metre-high metal cones that can be seen from far away. Thanks to an ingenious solution involving perforated metal, they seem like columns of light when seen at night or in the sunlight.

The fountain has become a favourite place for kids to meet and hang out. The precinct itself enables freedom of movement, either by bike or on foot. Although its design is plain and unassuming and the cost of construction was low, the precinct is held in great favour, and has become one of the most popular open spaces in Landskrona.

Ein eindrucksvolles Ensemble skulpturaler Objekte, bei Tag wie in der Nacht: Die Kegel aus perforiertem Metall tauchen Landskronas Bibliotheksplatz nachts in ein geheimnisvolles Licht.

The cones of perforated metal at the precinct of Landskrona library are a striking sculptural ensemble at any time of day, but are most effective at night, when they bathe the space in mysterious light.

Landskrona Library Square, Sweden
Client: Municipality of Landskrona
Landscape architect: Monika Gora
Assistant: Veronika Borg
Limited competition: 1997
Size: 3,599 square metres
Construction: 1999
Light planning: Lars Bylund
Costs: SEK 1.5 million, SEK 500 per square metre

Jeder Raum hat seinen Platz

Every space has a place

Thorbjörn Andersson

The story of Sergels Torg, a plaza in Stockholm, pinpoints three fundamental factors that are of significance for urban design. The first is that the design of a city must be regarded as an ongoing process, one that people need time to become acquainted with. After all, cities do not develop overnight, nor can urban space design change in the same way that fashions come and go.

The second factor is that urban spaces have to relate to their surroundings (context) and to their history (depth of time), not for antiquarian reasons per se but because memories create identity, and context creates understanding. Urban spaces that are designed rather than understood run the risk of being reduced to products, and a city that is composed of products will have difficulty establishing itself as a life habitat. It is simply hard to feel at home in such a place.

The third factor is that open space design in cities has a strong impact on over-all city renewal. In contrast to buildings, open space is used by everyone and is generally also financed with taxpayers' money. It thus has an exclusive ability to engage the attention of people at large, as the example of Sergels Torg will show, and can thus act as a force of urban renewal.

Sergels Torg, Stockholm. When Sergels Torg was inaugurated in 1974, the creation of the plaza was promoted as world class news. Nowhere else did a more modern plaza exist. Sergels Torg was nothing less than a monument of the late era of the modern movement, and came to symbolise the renewal of the whole city, perhaps indeed the whole era. Designed to keep traffic away from the people, it featured modern new forms with sweeping curves and bold lines, as well as paving with a striking black and white

Lebensraum Stadt – Die Gestaltung öffentlicher Räume weckt das Interesse der Bürger und treibt die städtische Erneuerung voran.

Cities as a life habitat – By awakening active interest, changes in the design of public open spaces can foster overall urban renewal.

triangular pattern. A composition with a tall crystal sculpture by the artist Edvin Öhrström stood at its side, along with a fountain with the shape of a super-ellipse, a new form created by the Danish mathematician Piet Hein. The super-ellipse was a hybrid between a quadrangle and an ellipse, and represented new ways of thinking as well as freedom from the burden of the old city and its rectilinear grid. The plaza did not hold much vegetation but consisted of modern materials, such as concrete, water and free-flowing air. Five high-rise buildings were erected on the northern side of Sergels Torg, and when the mayor Yngve Larsson held his speech at the inauguration, he expressed his optimism at what had been achieved, describing the high-rise buildings as five trumpet-blasts saluting the new era.

The plaza, however, soon fell into disgrace. It was desolate, windy and almost hostile. The Stockholmers did not find themselves at ease there. Instead, it became a gathering place for prostitutes and drug dealers. The black and white paving became a symbol of despair, and during the eighties was used several times in detective films to suggest an atmosphere of terror and criminality. The plaza was nick-named "the slab", and became associated with a rough downtown quarter abandoned by its previous inhabitants. To this very day, comparatively few apartments are left at the very most central part of Stockholm.

A strong wave of criticism rose. A 19th-century city that was cosier in character and smaller in scale once stood at the spot of the modern new plaza, characterised by charming houses and picturesque little streets, as people would say. In comparison to the new city, the Klara blocks, as

Die Geschichte des Stockholmer Platzes Sergels Torg beleuchtet drei Grundwerte der Städteplanung. Erstens muß die Gestaltung einer Stadt ein ständiger Prozeß sein, ein Prozeß, an den wir uns gewöhnen müssen. Eine Stadt entsteht nicht von heute auf morgen. Deshalb kann auch die Gestaltung urbaner Räume nicht einfach verändert werden, wenn die Mode sich ändert. Zweitens müssen sich urbane Räume in irgendeiner Weise auf ihre Umgebung, den Kontext, und ihre Geschichte, die Zeittiefe, beziehen – nicht so sehr aus nostalgischen Gründen, sondern weil Erinnerungen Identität schaffen und Kontext Verständnis. Urbane Räume, die nur gestaltet aber nicht verstanden werden, laufen Gefahr, nur noch Produkt zu sein. Eine Stadt aber, die nur aus Produkten besteht, wird sich nur schwer als Lebensraum etablieren können. Man kann sich eben an einem solchen Ort nicht leicht zu Hause fühlen. Drittens hat die Gestaltung offener Räume in Städten große Auswirkungen auf die Erneuerung der Stadt insgesamt. Mehr noch als ihre Gebäude werden die offenen Räume von allen genutzt – und meist auch mit Steuergeldern, also von allen, finanziert. Die Gestaltung offener Räume weckt also, wie das Beispiel Sergels Torg zeigt, viel stärker das aktive Interesse der Bürger und kann daher als Antriebskraft für die städtische Erneuerung eingesetzt werden.

Sergels Torg, Stockholm. Als der Sergels Torg 1974 eingeweiht wurde, ging die Nachricht um die Welt. Nirgendwo sonst gab es einen so modernen Platz. Sergels Torg war nichts weniger als ein Denkmal der Spätmoderne und wurde zum Symbol für die Erneuerung der gesamten Stadt, vielleicht sogar einer ganzen Ära. Die Verkehrsströme liefen hier völlig voneinander getrennt. Der Platz war geprägt durch neue, moderne Formen mit weit ausholenden Kurven und kräftigen Linien. Das Pflaster wies ein auffallend schwarzweißes Dreiecksmuster auf. An der Seite standen eine hohe Kristallskulptur von Edvin Öhrström und ein Brunnen. Der Brunnen hatte die Form einer Superellipse – eine neue Form geschaffen von dem dänischen Mathematiker Piet Hein. Diese Superellipse war eine Mischung aus einem Viereck und einer Ellipse und repräsentierte damals gewissermaßen die neue Denkweise und die Befreiung von der Last der alten Stadt und ihres viereckigen Rasters. Der Platz wies kaum Bepflanzung auf, sondern bestand, so könnte man sagen, aus eher modernen Materialien: Beton, Wasser und ungehindert strömender Luft. An der Nordseite des Sergels Torg entstanden fünf Hochhäuser. Bei der Einweihung beschrieb Bürgermeister

1974, im Jahr seiner Einweihung, galt Sergels Torg in Stockholm als ein Musterprojekt der Spätmoderne. Errichtet wurde dieser Platz in dem ehemals dichtbebauten Stadtviertel Klara. Doch die Freude über die moderne Gestaltung währte nicht lange, schon Mitte der 80er Jahre diente er als triste Kulisse für Kriminalfilme. Das Pflaster mit dem schwarzweißen Dreiecksmuster galt als Sinnbild des desolaten Zustands. In die Diskussion um den Wiederumbau schaltete sich auch das Stockholmer Architekturmuseum mit Protestbuttons ein.

In 1974, when Sergels Torg was inaugurated, the plaza in the formerly densely-built district of Klara was regarded as a monument of the late era of the modern movement. The optimism its modern design called forth did not last, however, and by the mid-eighties it had become a suitably desolate setting for detective films, its black and white paving a symbol of despair. A new phase of remodelling was suggested to alleviate the situation, but called for the protests on the part of the Stockholm Museum of Architecture.

Yngve Larsson in seiner Rede seine optimistischen Gefühle hinsichtlich dessen, was er und die Städteplaner erreicht hatten. Die fünf Hochhäuser bezeichnete er als fünf Trompetenstöße zur Begrüßung einer neuen Ära. Der Platz fiel jedoch bald in Ungnade. Er war verlassen, windig und fast abweisend. Die Stockholmer fühlten sich dort nicht wohl, statt dessen bevölkerten ihn Prostituierte und Drogendealer. Das schwarzweiße Muster wurde zum Symbol der Verzweiflung und diente in den Kriminalfilmen der 80er Jahre immer wieder als Mittel, eine Atmosphäre von Kriminalität und Schrecken herzustellen. Der Platz bekam den Spitznamen »die Platte« und wurde immer mehr ein Symbol für die desolate Innenstadt, deren Bewohner längst in andere Gegenden gezogen waren. Bis heute gibt es relativ wenige Wohnungen in diesem zentral gelegenen Teil Stockholms. Die Kritik wurde immer lauter. Dort, wo nun die neue Innenstadt mit ihrem modernen Platz entstanden war, befand sich im 19. Jahrhundert ein entschieden gemütlicherer und kleiner dimensionierter Stadtteil mit alten Häusern, Gassen und pittoresken kleinen Straßen. Im Klara-Viertel, wie dieser alte Stadtteil genannt wurde, verbrachten viele Künstler und Schriftsteller ihre Zeit in den Cafés. Als Lebensraum hatte er jedoch auch seine Mängel, denn er war dicht bevölkert und die sanitären Bedingungen waren schlecht. Sergels Torg war die Antwort der Planungsexperten und Politiker auf diese Mißstände. Die Stadtverödung um den Sergels Torg führte jedoch erneut zu der entschiedenen Forderung nach einer weiteren Veränderung. Die alte Form städtischen Lebens und die Werte dieser alten, nostalgischen Art von Stadt galten wieder als Vorbild. Die Menschen waren entsetzt darüber, wie massiv man in den alten Bestand eingegriffen hatte. So entstand ein Film mit dem Titel »Erinnern Sie sich an diese Stadt«, der landesweit im Fernsehen ausgestrahlt wurde. Er zeigte alte Fotografien und konfrontierte die dadurch geweckten Erinnerungen mit der Nacktheit der neuen Umgebung. Die modernen Architekten wurden als rücksichtslos und totalitär dargestellt. Nun war es also an der Zeit für eine erneute umfassende Veränderung des Sergels Torg. Die Stadtväter beauftragten fünf Architekturbüros, Vor-

the old part of city was known, had an active street life, and many artists and writers gathered at the cafés. Nevertheless, as a human habitat it had its limitations, being crowded and of low sanitary standard. Sergels Torg was the reaction of planners and politicians to this state of affairs.

In the meantime, the new type of urban desolation around Sergels Torg began to generate strong demands for yet another change. The old type of city life and the picturesque values associated with it were called for, and people remained upset about the massive demolition that had made way for the plaza. The national television network broadcast a documentary titled *Do You Remember That Town,* which juxtaposed old photos that awoke old memories with others that showed the nakedness of the new environment, depicting the modern architects as ruthless and totalitarian. The time had obviously come for another crucial change to Sergels Torg. The city fathers accordingly commissioned five architectural practices to draw up proposals that would accord more space to humans and greenery, and less to traffic.

So far, this is not an unusual story. Many Swedish and foreign city cores have ended up the same way or been treated with the same crudeness. Even a city like Los Angeles once had classical city qualities, formed by turn-of-the-century ideals rather than the uncompromising urban renewal visions of the modern movement. The remarkable thing about Sergels Torg is, however, that just as the new and radical phase of remodelling was about to take place, loud opinions began to made themselves felt, voiced by people who were born in the sixties or later, and whose memories and experience were thus formed by the modern Sergels Torg and not by the old Klara

Architekt David Helldén entwarf Sergels Torg 1960-1967. Seine Perspektivskizze zeigt seine Vision des sozialen Lebens auf dem Platz.
Der 38 Meter hohe Kristallobelisk von Edwin Öhrström steht inmitten eines Brunnens mit der Grundform einer Superellipse.

The architect David Helldén designed Sergels Torg between 1960 and 1967. The perspective view reveals his idea of how social life would unfold at the plaza.
The 38-metre-high crystal obelisk is surrounded by a fountain with the shape of a super-ellipse.

blocks. If we are to change Sergels Torg again, how should this change be made? What about the memories of the younger generation and the city they grew up in? The Museum of Architecture in Stockholm promptly made protest buttons featuring the black and white triangles of the plaza's infamous pavement pattern, and was made "Museum of the Year" for its involvement in the issue. Some people thought the plaza should be listed as a historical monument, while others opined that Sergels Torg was a wound that had finally healed, so why tear it open again? The outcome was that without any actual physical changes, Sergels Torg was suddenly taken to the hearts of the people of Stockholm. As a result, it is now being gently remodelled in a programme that began in 1998, involving relatively modest measures, such as a new lighting program, the replacement of worn materials, and certain traffic adjustments.

The story of Sergels Torg shows that downtown renewal has to take the history and the context of a place into consideration. These form the often-invisible values that constitute life itself, and which are as important as very substantial assets as a park bench in the sun. Few have described this matter better than Italo Calvino in his book *The Invisible Cities,* in which he explores the multi-layered fabric of memories and past events that make up cities. The story of Sergels Torg also shows that thoughts and ideas travel almost as fast as fashion, and that changes in urban design and landscape architecture take place on a slower scale, with the result that this discrepancy can create conflicts between idea and built reality. In my office, I and my colleague PeGe Hillnge have tried to apply this insight to urban design, our field of specialisation.

Sergels Torgs charakteristisches Pflaster dient immer noch als Bühne für städtisches Leben aller Art, darunter aber auch unerwünschtes. Das zunehmend schlechte Image des Platzes brachte allgemein den öffentlichen Raum Stockholms in die Debatte.

The paving that is so characteristic of Sergels Torg still serves as a setting for all aspects of urban life, including undesirable ones. The increasingly poor image of the plaza sparked off a broad discussion about the role that open space plays in Stockholm.

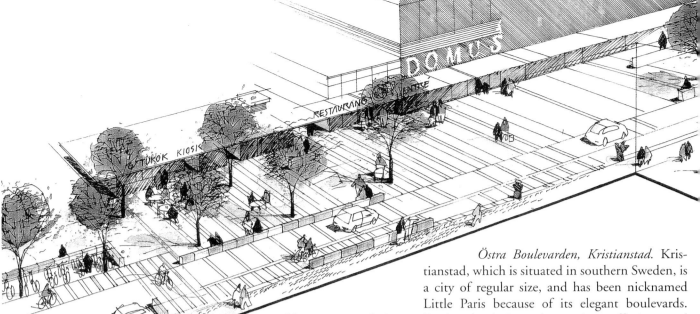

Kristianstad im Süden Schwedens war für ihre eleganten Boulevards bekannt. Zunehmender Autoverkehr in den 60er und 70er Jahren vereinnahmte jedoch die Straßen. Durch ein neues Verkehrskonzept konnte Östra Boulevarden zu einer Einbahnstraße mit eingeschränktem Verkehr umgestaltet werden. Gestreiftes Pflaster quer zur Fahrtrichtung verlangsamt, während parallel laufende Mauern und vier Skulpturen von Pål Svensson den Verlauf der Straße betonen. Entwurf: FFNS

Kristianstad, situated in southern Sweden, used to be famed for its elegant boulevards, but its reputation was tarred in the sixties and seventies when the thoroughfares became increasingly choked with traffic. A traffic re-organisation scheme was accordingly introduced, creating the possibility to make Östra Boulevarden into a one-way, traffic-only street. Traverse strips of paving now slow down traffic, while walls and four granite sculptures by Pål Svensson emphasise the one-way direction of the street. Design: FFNS

schläge auszuarbeiten. Die grundlegende Vorgabe war, Menschen und Bepflanzung mehr Raum zu geben und den Verkehr zurückzudrängen.

So weit keine ungewöhnliche Geschichte. Die City vieler Städte in Schweden wie in anderen Ländern hat das gleiche Schicksal erlitten und wurde genauso gefühllos behandelt. Selbst eine Stadt wie Los Angeles besaß einst die klassischen Eigenschaften einer Stadt und entsprach mehr den um die Jahrhundertwende entstandenen Idealvorstellungen als den kompromißlosen Stadterneuerungsplänen der Modernisten. Das Bemerkenswerte am Sergels Torg ist jedoch, daß sich nun, da eine erneute, radikale Umwandlung vor der Tür stand, eine neue Stimme Gehör verschaffte: Die in und nach den 60er Jahren Geborenen, deren Erinnerungen und Stadtbild von dem modernen Sergels Torg geprägt sind und die das alte Klara-Viertel nicht mehr gekannt haben. Wenn wir jetzt den Sergels Torg wieder umbauen, wie müssen wir uns dann ändern? Wie steht es mit den Erinnerungen der jüngeren Generation und der Stadt, in der sie aufgewachsen ist? Das Architekturmuseum in Stockholm gab passenderweise Protestbuttons mit den schwarzweißen Dreiecken des berühmtberüchtigten Pflasters des Platzes heraus und erhielt für sein Engagement in dieser Sache prompt die Auszeichnung »Museum des Jahres«. Einige fanden sogar, der Platz solle unter Denkmalschutz gestellt werden. Andere dagegen hielten es für unsinnig, den Sergels Torg jetzt wieder aufzureißen, nachdem diese Wunde endlich verheilt war. Ergebnis der Debatte war, daß der Sergels Torg, ehe überhaupt irgendwelche Veränderungen vorgenommen worden waren, den Stockholmern plötzlich lieb und teuer war. Seit 1998 wird er nun durch relativ geringfügige Maßnahmen, wie zum Beispiel ein neues Beleuchtungsprogramm, Austausch abgenutzter Materialien und bestimmte Verkehrsanpassungen, auf sanfte Weise umgestaltet.

Die Geschichte vom Sergels Torg zeigt, daß bei der Innenstadterneuerung Geschichte und Kontext berücksichtigt werden müssen. Sie schaffen die oft unsichtbaren Werte, die das Leben selbst ausmachen und die ebenso wichtig sind wie zum Beispiel eine Parkbank in der Sonne. Kaum jemand

Östra Boulevarden, Kristianstad. Kristianstad, which is situated in southern Sweden, is a city of regular size, and has been nicknamed Little Paris because of its elegant boulevards. During the sixties and seventies, traffic increased to the extent that not much of the boulevard character was left at certain places. A traffic re-organisation scheme was introduced, creating the possibility to make Östra Boulevarden into a one-way, traffic-only street. We were entrusted with its design, in which we used broad, solid granite walls to emphasise the boulevard's historical direction, as well as traverse strips of paving to slow down traffic. On this project we worked together with the sculptor Pål Svensson, who contributed four granite closet-shaped sculptures to line the street. Östra Boulevarden was inaugurated in the summer of 1999.

Knutpunkt Hjalmar, Gothenburg. Gothenburg, which is situated on the west coast of Sweden, is the country's second largest city, and the site of the Knutpunkt Hjalmar project, which was inaugurated in 1998. Knutpunkt means junction, an apt description as it is a place where 60,000 people change from one form of transportation to another every day. Knutpunkt Hjalmar can be described as a gigantic bus stop with a complicated movement pattern of cars, buses, trolleys, bicycle-riders and pedestrians. As a site, it had only vague contours with regard to history and context, since very little existed of the two. We sketched a large triangular shape and divided it into two, making the northern half a formal grouping of ash trees that we called 'the forest', whereby the southern half was paved in black and white stripes and named 'the square'. We elevated car traffic up onto a bridge, placing pedestrian and bicycle traffic beneath, and inserted five funnels of perforated sheet metal into a slit in the middle of the bridge. The light funnels, as we called them, not only introduce light into the pedestrian underpass, but also ease orientation and add character to this urban space. The idea was inspired by the similarly-shaped water towers that are often seen in Swedish cities, where they serve as landmarks in addition to their more functional purpose.

Kvarnholmsplan, Norrköping. Norrköping, which is situated a two-hours'-drive south of Stockholm, is one of the larger cities in Sweden. It entered a downward spiral in the seventies, when several important industries left town, causing high unemployment and related problems. The other side of the coin, however, was that Norrköping inherited a derelict downtown industrial landscape that summarised 400 years of the city's history. This brownfield area is situated on the banks of the Motala Ström river, the lifeline of the many different industries that have existed at the site over the years. We designed the front plaza at this historical area, which is called Holmens Bruk and which is now filled with such cultural establishments as a science centre, a concert hall, a museum of labour and a university. The plaza, which is known as Kvarnholmsplan, is half land, half water, whereby a wide rounded line divides the two.

In designing the plaza, we sought to recall the past of the site by making no use of vegetation but concentrating instead on the kind of materials that were once common at the industrial environment, namely stone, brick, iron and water. An underground garage has been built beneath the plaza, and is entered by driving down a ramp

hat dies so gut beschrieben wie Italo Calvino in seinem Buch »Die unsichtbaren Städte«. Der Autor untersucht hier das vielschichtige Gewebe von Erinnerungen und Ereignissen in der Vergangenheit, die jede Stadt ausmachen. Die Geschichte vom Sergels Torg zeigt aber auch, daß Gedanken und Ideen sich schnell verändern, fast so wie die Mode, während sich Stadt- und Landschaftsplanung nur langsam bewegen. Durch diese Zeitverzögerung können Konflikte zwischen den Vorstellungen und der gebauten Wirklichkeit entstehen. Ich habe in meinem Büro zusammen mit meinem Kollegen PeGe Hillnge versucht, diese Erfahrung in der Stadtgestaltung, unserem Spezialgebiet, aufzugreifen.

Östra Boulevarden, Kristianstad. Kristianstad ist eine Stadt mittlerer Größe in Südschweden, die wegen ihrer eleganten Boulevards den Spitznamen Klein-Paris erhalten hat. In den 60er und 70er Jahren nahm der Verkehr so zu, daß schließlich an vielen Stellen von dem ursprünglichen Boulevardcharakter nicht mehr viel übrig blieb. Durch eine Verkehrsumstrukturierung wurde es jedoch möglich, den Östra Boulevarden zu einer Einbahnstraße nur für den langsamen Verkehr umzugestalten. Wir haben hier breite, massive Granitmauern verwendet, um die Verkehrsrichtung der Straße hervorzuheben. Durch ein gestreiftes Pflaster in Querrichtung wird dagegen der Verkehr verlangsamt. Bei diesem Projekt haben wir mit dem Bildhauer Pål Svensson zusammengearbeitet, der vier schrankförmige Granitskulpturen schuf, die in Richtung der Straße verlaufen. Der Östra Boulevarden wird im Sommer 1999 fertiggestellt sein.

Knutpunkt Hjalmar, Göteborg. Göteborg, an der Westküste, ist die zweitgrößte Stadt Schwedens. Hier haben wir an dem Projekt Knutpunkt Hjalmar, das 1998 übergeben wurde, gearbeitet. Knutpunkt bedeutet Knotenpunkt. Hier verweilen täglich 60 000 Menschen einige Minuten, wenn sie umsteigen müssen. Man könnte Knutpunkt Hjalmar als eine gigantische Bushaltestelle bezeichnen mit einem komplizierten Gewirr von Autos, Bussen, Straßenbahnen, Radfahrern und Fußgängern. Bezüglich Geschichte und Kontext war hier nur wenig vorhanden, so daß sich kaum etwas daraus ableiten ließ. Wir entwarfen ein großes Dreieck, das wir in zwei Teile zerlegten. Der nördliche Teil erhielt eine Gruppe von Eschen, die wir den Wald nannten. Der südliche Teil wurde in schwarzweißen Streifen gepflastert und wurde zu einem Platz. Der Autoverkehr wurde über eine Brücke geführt, der Bereich unter der Brücke gehört Fußgängern und Radfahrern. Die Brücke wird durch fünf trichterförmige Lichtschächte aus perforiertem

Stahlblech angekündigt. Diese Lichtschächte versorgen die Fußgängerunterführung durch einen Schlitz in der Mitte der Brücke mit Licht. Sie sind jedoch auch Gesten in diesem urbanen Raum, Gesten, die bei der Orientierung helfen und dem Raum einen eigenen Charakter verleihen sollen. Die Idee stammt von den ähnlich geformten Wassertürmen, die man oft in schwedischen Städten sehen kann, wo sie neben ihrer eigentlichen Funktion auch als Orientierungspunkte dienen.

Kvarnholmsplan, Norrköping. Norrköping, etwa zwei Stunden mit dem Auto südlich von Stockholm gelegen, ist eine der größeren schwedischen Städte. Die Stadt geriet in den 70er Jahren in eine Abwärtsspirale, als mehrere wichtige Industrien der Stadt den Rücken kehrten, was zu hoher Arbeitslosigkeit und den damit verbundenen Problemen führte. Die andere Seite der Medaille war jedoch, daß Norrköping nun über eine ungenutzte alte Industrielandschaft mitten in der Stadt verfügen konnte, in der sich 400 Jahre Stadtgeschichte widerspiegelten. Sie erstreckte sich entlang der Ufer des Flusses Motala Ström, der die Lebensader der verschiedenen Industrien bildete, die sich hier über die Jahre befanden. Wir haben den Platz am vorderen Eingang zu diesem geschichtsträchtigen Gebiet, genannt Holmens Bruk, gestaltet. Holmens Bruk beherbergt heute zahlreiche kulturel-

Den Knotenpunkt Hjalmar in Göteborg passieren täglich 60 000 Menschen, die hier ein-, aus- oder umsteigen. FFNS entwarf ein großes Dreieck als Grundform, das in zwei Hälften geteilt wurde. Die nördliche erhielt ein Wäldchen aus Eschen, die südliche ein schwarzweißes Streifenpflaster. Eine Brücke trennt Autos von Fußgängern und Radfahrern. Fünf trichterförmige Lichtschächte beleuchten die Unterführung, dienen aber zugleich als neues Wahrzeichen. Ihre Form erinnert ein wenig an die Svampen (Pilz) genannten Wassertürme, die im ganzen Land Orientierung bieten.

Every day, 60,000 commuters change from one form of transportation to another at the Hjalmar junction in Gothenburg. In redesigning the site, FFNS sketched a large triangular shape and divided it into two, making the northern half a formal grouping of ash trees, and paving the southern half in black and white stripes. They also elevated car traffic onto a bridge, placing pedestrian and bicycle traffic below. Five funnels introduce light into the pedestrian underpass facilitating orientation. The idea was inspired by similarly-shaped water towers common throughout the country.

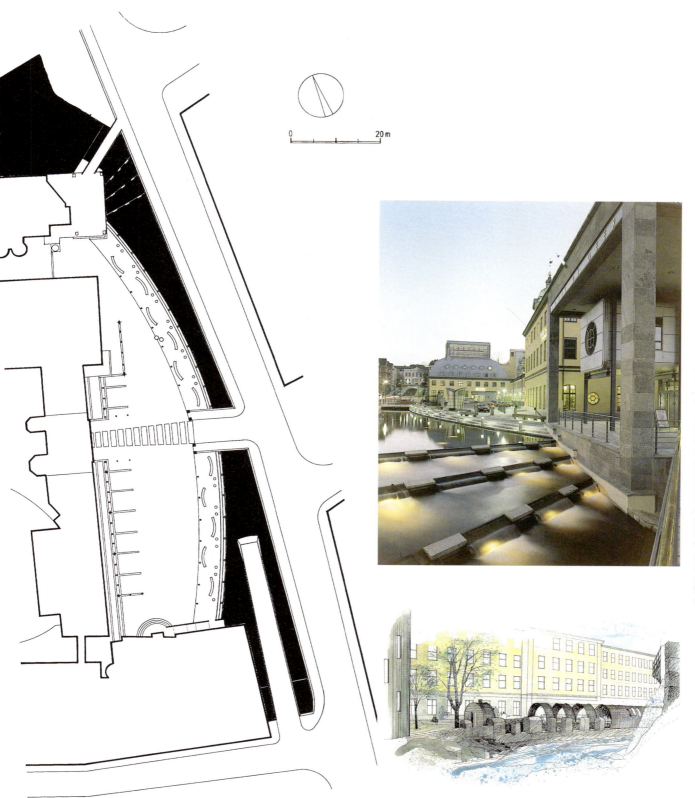

Norrköping liegt südlich von
Stockholm und ist für schwedi-
sche Verhältnisse eine größere
Stadt. Heute besitzt die Stadt
eine ungenutzte Industrielandschaft am Fluß Motala mit einer 400jährigen Geschichte.
FFNS gestaltete Holmens
Bruk, einen Eingangsplatz zur
alten Industriezone. Der Platz
ist halb Land, halb Wasser, mit
einem breiten Kreissegment
als Trennlinie. Eine riesige
Röhre, die früher als Öllager
diente, wurde aufgeschnitten,
damit sie begehbar wird und
den Blick auf den Wasserfall
freigibt.

Norrköping, situated south of
Stockholm, is one of the larger
cities in Sweden, and features
a derelict industrial landscape
called Holmens Bruk on the
banks of the Motala River.
FFNS designed the front plaza
at this historical area, which
can look back on a past of 400
years. The plaza is now half
land, half water, divided by a
wide rounded line. A huge
steel cylinder formerly used to
store oil was cut open, thus
providing access to the waterfall existing at the site and
opening up views of it.

le Aktivitäten, darunter ein Wissenschaftszentrum, eine Konzerthalle, ein Museum der Arbeit und eine Universität. Der Platz, Kvarnholmsplan, ist halb Land, halb Wasser. Die Trennlinie zwischen beiden bildet ein breites Kreissegment. Bei der Gestaltung des Platzes haben wir versucht, die historischen Werte dieser Umgebung aufzunehmen, indem wir weniger mit Grünflächen als mit den Materialien gearbeitet haben, die für diese Industrielandschaft typisch waren: Stein, Ziegel, Eisen und Wasser. Unter dem Platz befindet sich eine Tiefgarage, die Zufahrtsrampe führt die einfahrenden Autos unter die Wasseroberfläche. Hat der Besucher einmal Holmens Bruk betreten, geht er auf eine Felsplatte vor einem riesigen Wehr. Am Rande der Felsplatte liegt, parallel zu diesem Wehr, ein Stahlzylinder mit 3,5 Meter Durchmesser und 60 Meter Länge, der früher als Öllager verwendet wurde. Die Röhre, wie wir diesen Zylinder immer nennen, blockierte den Zugang zu der Felsplatte und den Blick auf den Wasserfall. In unserem Entwurf schnitten wir die Röhre auf wie einen gebratenen Fisch, damit das Licht einfallen und die Röhre begehbar gemacht werden konnte. Damit schufen wir öffentlichen Zugang und freien Blick auf das Wehr. Wir konnten also ein historisches Objekt erhalten und ihm gleichzeitig eine neue Funktion geben. Der Wasserfall und die dramatisch wirkende Schlucht verleihen dieser Umgebung einen ganz eigenen Charakter. Wie schon bei mehreren anderen Projekten haben wir auch hier mit dem Lichtdesigner Mikael Hallbert zusammengearbeitet. Das Projekt wurde 1998 fertiggestellt.

Diese vier Projekte zeigen aus verschiedenen Blickwinkeln, wie die Gestaltung offener Räume zur Verbesserung der Qualität des urbanen Lebens insgesamt beitragen kann. Norrköping war eine heruntergekommene Stadt mit schwach ausgeprägtem Selbstbewußtsein. Die Erneuerung von Holmens Bruk hat den Bürgern etwas von ihrem Glauben in und Stolz auf ihre Stadt zurückgegeben. Knutpunkt Hjalmar liegt in einem Teil von Göteborg, der jegliche Art von Freiraumgestaltung vermissen ließ. Der neue Platz hat den Teil der Stadt bereits zum neuen Stadtgespräch im positiven Sinne gemacht. Und Kristianstad hatte einen Teil seiner optischen Identität verloren, als die Alleebäume des Östra Boulevarden zum größten Teil entfernt wurden. Jetzt wurde dieses Wahrzeichen von Kristianstad wieder im neuen Gewand hergestellt. Das Beispiel Sergels Torg zeigt auf der anderen Seite, daß der Erfolg nicht gewährleistet ist. Wenn die entscheidenden Faktoren Kontext und Zeittiefe nicht berücksichtigt werden, kann einem Entwurf eine nur kurze Lebensdauer beschieden sein.

that takes the cars below the level of the water. Once inside the Holmens Bruk area, the visitor approaches a shelf opposite a large waterfall that thunders into a gorge. A steel cylinder, 3.5 metres in diameter and 60 metres long, lies, parallel to the waterfall at the edge of this shelf, and was formerly used to store oil. The tube, as we came to call it, blocked access to the shelf and the view of the waterfall. We therefore slit it open like a cooked fish to let in the light, and created a passage through its length to provide public access and views of the waterfall. A historical object has thus been preserved and given a new function, while the waterfall and the dramatic gorge provide it a setting that is strong in character. In this project and several others, we worked with the light designer Mikael Hallbert. The project itself was inaugurated in 1998.

These four projects show how open space projects can be used to improve the over-all quality of urban life. Norrköping was a run-down town of little self-confidence until the Holmens Bruk renewal gave the citizens back their pride and their belief in their city. Knutpunkt Hjalmar, for its part, is situated in an area of Gothenburg that lacked almost any kind of environmental assets, but the new square has made it the talk of the town.

As for Kristianstad, it lost part of its visual identity when a vital section of the street trees along Östra Boulevarden were removed, but this trademark of the city has now been restored. In contrast, the example of Sergels Torg shows that success is not automatic, and that a design will be short-lived if the crucial factors of context and history are not taken into consideration.

Der neue Heuvelplein in Tilburg

The new Heuvelplein in Tilburg

"Vedute della città ideale", views of an ideal city, is the collective title of a series of paintings attributed to the school of Piero della Francesca (about 1480). In those days ideal views of towns were a favourite subject. At the height of the Italian Renaissance, painters were also architects and urban planners, creating an aesthetic image of the city's ideal composition. These pictures have greatly influenced our conception of how a square should look: an empty open space between or beside buildings, usually surrounded on several sides by walls of urban fabric. Sight lines, dimensions, proportions and ornamentation are important components of the ideal image. In practice, things are often more unruly.

At least in The Netherlands, squares developed in a more or less organic way. Before they were architecturally designed, they had already existed as a result of the grown infrastructure. Or else they evolved because other functions had become meaningless. How De Heuvel came about in Tilburg, an industrial city in the southern Netherlands, was no different. The designation of industrial city in combination with the history of this square are typical for the growth of medium-sized Netherlandish cities. The name of De Heuvel (the hill) refers to its origins. The actual city of Tilburg arose at a much later date. De Heuvel originated as a so-called "heerdgang", a triangular public place at the crossroads of various roads. In the course of time, village structures gradually developed, first an inn and a few tradespeople to serve the travellers, then a church and later houses, lined up in a row along the roads. The city of Tilburg is a conglomeration of several such crossroads and rows of houses, an accretion of different village cores, the most im-

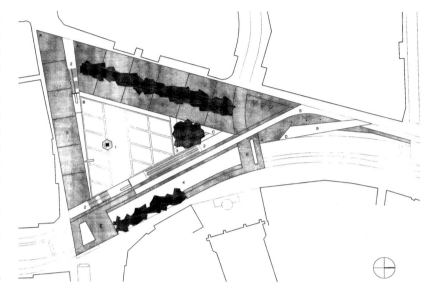

»Vedute della città ideale«, Ansichten der idealen Stadt, lautet der Sammeltitel für eine Reihe von Gemälden, die der Scuola di Piero della Francesca (um 1480) zugeschrieben werden. Seinerzeit waren ideale Stadtansichten ein beliebtes Bildthema. Auf dem Höhepunkt der italienischen Renaissance waren die Maler gleichzeitig Architekten und Städtebauer und schufen als solche ein ästhetisches Bildnis der kompositorisch idealen Stadt. Diese Bilder haben in hohem Maße unsere Vorstellung darüber beeinflußt, wie ein Platz auszusehen hat: Ein offener, unbebauter Raum zwischen oder neben Bauwerken, der meist auf mehreren Seiten von Stadtwänden umschlossen ist. Sichtlinien, Maß, Proportionen und Ornamente waren wichtige Elemente des Idealbilds. Die Praxis ist häufig widerspenstiger. Die Plätze haben sich, zumindest in den Niederlanden, anders entwickelt, auf mehr oder weniger organische Weise. Bevor sie noch entworfen wurden, existierten sie bereits als Ergebnis einer gewachsenen Infrastruktur, oder sie entstanden dadurch, daß andere Funktionen bedeutungslos geworden waren. Die Entstehung des Heuvel (Hügel) in Tilburg, einer Industrie-

Willem Oomens

Einst Kreuzungspunkt, heute Zentrum. Die Rekonstruktion des dreieckigen Platzes schuf Urbanität in dieser heterogenen Stadt.
Once a junction, now the centre of a city – the reconstruction of this triangular square symbolises urbanism.

Der neue Heuvel – früher ein offener dreieckiger Platz, der als Kreuzungspunkt verschiedener Wege diente, heute das urbane Zentrum der Stadt.

The new Heuvel – formerly an open triangular square that served as a junction of several roads, now the urban centre of a city.

stadt im Süden der Niederlande, war nicht anders. Die Bezeichnung Industriestadt in Kombination mit der Entstehungsgeschichte des Platzes ist charakteristisch für die Entwicklung einer mittelgroßen niederländischen Stadt. Der Heuvel verweist auf einen älteren Ursprung, während die eigentliche Entwicklung als Stadt erst viel später stattgefunden hat. Der Heuvel in Tilburg hat seinen Ursprung in einem sogenannten »heerdgang«, einem offenen, dreieckigen Ort, der als Kreuzungspunkt verschiedener Wege diente. Nach und nach haben sich daraus dörfliche Strukturen entwickelt, erst eine Herberge und einige Handwerksbetriebe für Reisende, danach eine Kirche und später Wohnhäuser, die sich bandförmig entlang der Zufahrtswege ansiedelten. Die Stadt Tilburg ist ein Konglomerat von verschiedenen Wegkreuzungen und Siedlungsbändern, ein Zusammenwuchs unterschiedlicher Dorfkerne, als deren bedeutendster der Heuvel bezeichnet werden kann. Dieses Zusammenwachsen verlieh dem Ort eine Urbanität, die für die einzelnen Dorfkerne neu war. Die Typologie der Stadt Tilburg kann als eine Ansammlung meist dreieckiger Plätze charakterisiert werden, die durch Achsen verbunden sind, auf die hin die schmalen, tiefen Parzellen ausgerichtet sind. Als »primus inter pares« wurde der Heuvel zum Mittelpunkt dieser neuen Stadt. Damit veränderte sich sein Charakter: Er war nun das Zentrum und die übrigen Elemente der Stadt wurden zur Peripherie. Der Heuvel symbolisiert die historische Authentizität der Stadt in seiner Eigenschaft als prominentester öffentlicher Raum.

An einen solchen Stadtraum werden Anforderungen gestellt: Aus seinem dörflichen Ursprung heraus soll der Ort Intimität, Geborgenheit und Gemütlichkeit ausstrahlen. Er soll kleinmaßstäblich sein und gleichzeitig als Treffpunkt dienen können. Diesen Charakter hatte er über lange Zeit hinweg, bis er Opfer seiner eigenen neuen Zentrumsfunktion wurde. Durch den immer stärker werdenden Verkehr, die Ausbreitung von Geschäften und Gastronomie und den damit zusammenhängenden Besucherstrom entstand ein immer größerer Druck. Widerspüchliche Bedürfnisse stießen aufeinander, die in einem anarchistischen Prozeß um die Vorherrschaft stritten. Die Gemeinde Tilburg erkannte dieses Problem und beauftragte das Büro Dirrix van Wylick Architekten damit, einen Vorschlag zur Rekonstruktion auszuarbeiten.

Das Büro hat nun nicht versucht, durch eine nostalgische, historische Erinnerung den Gang der Geschichte zu stoppen. Von Anfang an konzentrierte sich der Entwurf darauf, den Platz nicht nur in seiner wörtlichen,

portant of which is De Heuvel. This growing together created an urbanism new to the separate villages. The typology of Tilburg can be characterized as an assemblage of mostly triangular places that are connected by axes with long, narrow lots extending out from them. Being the "primus inter pares", De Heuvel became the centre of this new city, and the other former villages the periphery. In its capacity as a prominent public space, De Heuvel symbolises the historic authenticity of the city.

Many demands are made of such an urban space. To recall its village origins the square should radiate intimacy, shelter and coziness. It should be small in scale but also serve as a meeting place. De Heuvel did have these features for a long time, until it became a victim of its new function as a centre. This brought ever increasing traffic, the spread of shops and gastronomic establishments, and masses of visitors, creating more and more pressure. Contradictory needs conflicted with each other, struggling for domination in anarchy. When the municipality of Tilburg realised the problem it commissioned the Dirrix van Wylick architecture office to develop a proposal to reconstruct the square. The office did not try to stop the course of history with a nostalgic historical revival. Right from the start, the design concentrated on rebuilding the square with both its literal and symbolic significance. The problem was how to maintain its old visual significance as a meeting place while developing new dynamics.

The city square, at least if it is a product of history such as De Heuvel in Tilburg, is indeed perceived completely differently now. All new elements, such as traffic, large-scale loading areas,

Der neue Heuvel präsentiert sich urban, der historische, dreieckige Platzcharakter blieb erhalten. Die Kreuzung, als Treffpunkt gestaltet, entwickelt eine neue Dynamik. Auf der Ostseite des Platzes dominiert eine Terrassenzone, und die Statue von Willem II wacht über den ansonsten offen gehaltenen Platz.

The new Heuvel makes an urban impression; the historic triangular character of the junction was retained. The crossroads, designed as a meeting place, has developed new dynamics. The east side of the square features a terraced zone, and the statue of Willem II watches over what is otherwise an open area.

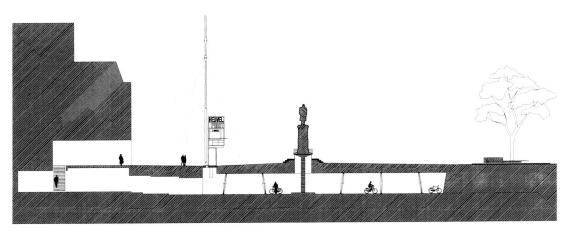

Die unterirdische Fahrradgara-
ge eignet sich für verschiedene
Zwecke, so daß auch vertikale
Verkehrsströme entstehen
können, die die Dynamik des
Platzes noch erhöhen.

The underground parking for
bicycles is also suited for various other uses, thus creating
vertical traffic flows that
further enhance the square's
dynamics.

sondern auch in seiner symbolischen Bedeutung zu rekonstruieren. Die Frage war, wie unter Beibehaltung der alten bildlichen Bedeutung des Platzes die Kreuzung als Treffpunkt gestaltet werden und eine neue, städtische Dynamik entwickeln werden könnte.

Regie als städtebauliche Entwurfsstrategie. Walter Benjamin schrieb einmal, daß sich innerhalb großer geschichtlicher Zeiträume mit der gesamten Lebensweise der menschlichen Gemeinschaft auch die Weise der sinnlichen Wahrnehmung ändert. Dies trifft auch auf die Wahrnehmung des niederländischen Platzes zu. Die wahren Freiräume unserer Zeit sind die stilisierten Verkehrsknotenpunkte, die landschaftlichen Plätze. Sie entsprechen in keiner Weise mehr dem Idealbild des Stadtraums, das in der Renaissance gezeichnet wurde.

Der Platz in der Stadt, zumindest wenn er wie der Heuvel in Tilburg ein Produkt der Geschichte ist, wird heute auf andere Weise wahrgenommen. Alle neuen Elemente, wie Verkehr, großmaßstäbliche Ladenzonen, Gastronomie und die immer neuen Besucherströme werden in zunehmendem Maße als lästig und unkontrollierbar empfunden. Sie wirken als Bedrohung für den historischen Ort. Die Wahrnehmung wird nicht von der Geschichte des Ortes geprägt, sondern von einer komplexen, chaotischen Struktur, die das Bild eines unentwirrbaren Knotens ergibt. Das Büro Dirrix van Wylick Architekten hat sich damit nicht zufrieden gegeben. Die Ursache für den Knoten liegt ihrer Ansicht nach nicht in der Komplexität der heutigen Urbanität, sondern im Rauschen, das damit einhergeht. Die Konfrontation von Verkehrs- und Aufenthaltsfunktion ist für sie genauso wichtig wie in der Vergangenheit und kann daher nicht als Problem gelten. Im Gegenteil, als die Essenz des Ortes. Diese Essenz muß neu gestaltet werden, indem der Leerraum umgeformt wird, oder anders gesagt, indem das Rauschen der Geschichte abgestellt wird und strategische Maßnahmen ergriffen werden, durch die die Konfrontation der verschiedenen Nutzungsmöglichkeiten nicht mehr als Konkurrenzproblem, sondern als eine neue faszinierende städtische Qualität erfahren wird. Dies erfordert in erster Linie eine Regie der verschiedenen Nutzungsmöglichkeiten und erst danach eine Gestaltung dieser Potentiale, da aus dem Zusammenhang heraus entschieden werden muß, welche visuelle Kraft die Einzelteile erhalten sollen.

Die städtische Dynamik des Platzes wird nicht nur durch die Lenkung der verschiedenen Verkehrsströme bestimmt, sondern auch durch die Behandlung der dazugehörigen Aufenthaltsfunktion. Man läuft und fährt

restaurants, fast food places and endless streams of visitors are increasingly seen as a nuisance and uncontrollable. They seem to threaten the historic square. Perception is not guided by the place's history but by a complex chaotic structure giving the impression of an indissoluble knot. The Dirrix van Wyck architecture office was not content with the status quo. In their opinion, the knot does not originate from the complexity of today's urbanism but from the rushing that accompanies it. Combining both the traffic and meeting place functions was as important to them as it had been in the past, and was therefore not the problem. On the contrary, it is the essence of the place. This essence needed to be restructured by reshaping the empty space, in other words, by turning off the rushing and taking strategic measures so that the coming together of various uses is no longer competitive but constitutes a fascinating new urban quality. First of all, this calls for staging the different possible uses. Only later should their potential be designed, because whatever visual power the individual elements have should be determined by the context.

The urban dynamics of the square are determined not only by directing the different streams of traffic but also by the treatment of its public function as a meeting place. People walk or ride across the square, sit down, or park their vehicles. These are functions directly related to the traffic flow. They need to be organised hierarchically, that is, staged so that the needs of each are met but they remain dependent on each other. To this end, the Heuvel was subdivided, renewed and reformulated. A new function shows at every turn, not in a blend but as a distinct component. This organisation of uses gives the square new con-

De Nieuwe Heuvel, Tilburg, The Netherlands
Client: City of Tilburg
Landscape architect: Dirrix van Wylick Architekten
Size: 10,000 square metres
Underground bicycle parking: 1,000 square metres
Costs: NLG 8,500,000

Die Statue von Willem II markiert die doppelte Nutzungsfunktion des Platzes: über- und
unterirdisch. Glasbausteine im
Sockel der Statue, der nachts
beleuchtet wird, verweisen auf
den darunterliegenden Raum.

The statue of Willem II marks
the twin functions of the square:
above and below ground.
Glass building stones in the
base of the statue, lit up
at night, indicate the space
underneath it.

über den Platz, man setzt sich und stellt sein Fahrzeug ab. Dies sind die Funktionen, die direkt mit dem Verkehrsstrom verbunden sind. Sie müssen in solcher Weise hierarchisch geordnet, also dirigiert werden, daß sie jeweils einzeln zu ihrem Recht kommen, aber voneinander abhängig bleiben. Zu diesem Zweck wurde der Heuvelplatz zergliedert, gereinigt und neu formuliert. Aus jeder Richtung zeigt sich eine neue Funktion, nicht als Amalgam, sondern als differenzierter Bestandteil. Durch diese Ordnung der Nutzungsqualitäten bekommt der Platz eine neue, zeitgemäße Dynamik und damit eine neue visuelle Wahrnehmung von Urbanität. Auf der Ostseite des Platzes dominiert eine exklusive Terrassenzone mit einer Hecke aus Linden. Diese Hecke hält das Platzzentrum frei von Verkehr, und die Statue von Willem II, einem früheren niederländischen Fürsten, wacht über den ansonsten leeren Platz und zugleich über eine unterirdische Fahrradgarage. Diese Fahrradgarage wird von der Rampe, den Treppen und den Glasbausteinstreifen markiert. Gleichzeitig verbindet dieser Fahrradkeller die Geschäftsbereiche an den Platzrändern. Er verdoppelt die Nutzungsfunktion des Platzes: über- und unterirdisch. Angesichts der heutigen logistischen Möglichkeiten eignet sich der unterirdische Raum für verschiedene Zwecke, so daß auch vertikale Verkehrsströme entstehen können, die die Dynamik des Platzes noch erhöhen. Auch die Einkaufspromenade an der Heuvelstraat trägt zur Dynamisierung des Platzes bei. Sowohl die horizontale Verbindung mit der Aufenthaltszone im Osten, als auch die vertikale Verbindung mit der Fahrradtiefgarage und den potentiellen neuen Funktionen intensivieren die Nutzung und damit die Komplexität der städtischen Situation, ohne chaotisch zu wirken.

Mit Hilfe der gewählten Hierarchie der Funktionen und deren entsprechender Gestaltung konnte die Komplexität teilweise aufgegliedert und transparent gemacht werden. Auch wenn sie noch nicht vollständig ergründet ist, ist sie doch faßbar und beherrschbar. Der Entwurf mußte zuerst ein Konzept, eine Strategie umreißen, bevor er ein neues visuelles Bild hervorbringen konnte. Der neue Heuvelplein ist eine neue 'Vedute della città ideale' geworden, genau wie damals ein Manifest darüber, wie Urbanität gestaltet werden kann. Die Vedute von Dirrix van Wylick Architekten unterscheidet sich im Wesentlichen nur in einem Punkt von dem Renaissancebild eines Piero della Francesca: Die Lebensbedingungen der menschlichen Gemeinschaft haben sich verändert. Aus diesem Grund hat der neue Heuvel genau diese Form bekommen.

temporary dynamics. Thus a new visual perception of urbanism evolves. The east side of the square is dominated by an exclusive terrace area with a linden hedge. The hedge keeps the centre of the square free of traffic. A statue of Willem II, an early Netherlandish prince, watches over the otherwise empty square and the underground parking for bicycles. The latter is indicated by a ramp, stairs and strips of glass building stones. It also connects the shopping areas on the edges of the square. It doubles the square's use: above and below ground. With today's logistic possibilities, the underground space is suited for various purposes, making vertical traffic flow possible and further enhancing the dynamics of the square. The shopping promenade in Heuvelstraat also contributes to making the square dynamic. The horizontal connection with the meeting place in the east, the vertical connection to the underground parking for bicycles and the potential new functions intensify the complexity of the urban situation without appearing chaotic.

With the help of a pre-established hierarchy of functions and their corresponding design, the complexity of the square could be somewhat broken up and made transparent. Even if it has not been completely penetrated, it can nevertheless be grasped and controlled. The design had to have a concept, a strategy, before it could provide a new visual image. The new Heuvelplein has become a new "veduta della città ideale", being just as much of a manifesto on urban design as the old Renaissance ones. The view by Dirrix van Wylick architects basically differs in only one point from those by Piero della Francesca's school: the living conditions of society have changed. That is why the new Heuvel was given precisely this form.

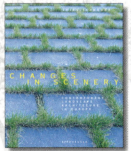   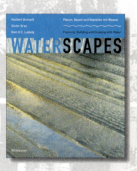

Authors
Photo credits
Translations
Impressum

Authors

Bjarne Aasen, born in 1933 in Trondheim, Norway, studied landscape architecture at the Norwegian Institute for Agriculture, where he lectured from 1976 to 1985. He is a professor for landscape architecture at the Faculty of Architecture at Trondheim University.

David Allen, a graduate in landscape architecture and MLI: Landscape Architecture, was a director and landscape architect at EDAW specialising in public realm design.

Thorbjörn Andersson, born in 1954, studied landscape architecture at the Alnarp Agricultural University in Sweden and at Berkeley, USA. He is both a chairman of FFNS, a co-operative group of landscape architects and founding editor of Utblick Landskap, now Area, the Swedish journal of landscape architecture.

Xavier Andreu Barrera, born in 1963, studied at the ETSAB. He has been in an office partnership specialised in landscape architecture with Jordi Bellmunt Chiva since 1992. He is also doing research at the university.

Andreu Arriola Madorell, born in 1956, studied architecture in Barcelona before opening up his own office in 1982 with Carmen Fiol. He held a guest professorship at the Academie van Bouwkunst van de HR&O in Rotterdam in 1992. Now he is professor at the E.T.S. d´Arquitectura de Barcelona.

Jordi Bellmunt Chiva was born in 1954. He studied at the ETSAB. He runs an office in partnership with Xavier Andreu Barrera in Barcelona. He has been teaching at the Polytechnical University of Catalonia since 1983.

Helga Benediktsdóttir, born in 1949 in Reykjavik, Island, studied architecture at the university of Southern California, Los Angeles, and Columbia University. Since 1987 she is a partner of the architects Elín Kjartansdóttir and Haraldur Örn Jónson in Verkstaedi 3 – architects, Reykjavik.

Bart Brands, born in 1962, studied at the Horticultural College in Boskoop and at the Department of Urban Development at the Academy of Architecture both in Rotterdam and Amsterdam. Since 1997 he has run his own practice, Karres and Brands, together with Sylvia Karres.

Jean-Pierre Charbonneau has been a consulting engineer for the city of Lyon, responsible for urban development planning and the design of public space, since 1989. He has been the technical adviser for urban design of the mayor of Saint-Etienne since 1996, and for the planning of the upper Seine "Mision Seine Amont" since 1997.

Roberto Collovà, born in 1943 in Sicily, studied architecture in Palermo. He is a professor at Palermo University, and has an office of his own in the same city. He

teaches in Barcelona, Las Palmas de Gran Canaria and Mendrisio, Switzerland.

Steve Christer, born in Blackfyne, Great Britain in 1960, went to the University of Newcastle upon Tyne from 1978 to 1981. In 1987, he found the Studio Granda in Reykjavik together with Margrét Hardardóttir. In 2000, he was guest tutor at the Universität Karlsruhe.

Carmen Fiol-Costa, born in 1956 in Barcelona, studied architecture at Columbia University, New York, and in Barcelona. She set up an office in partnership with Andreu Arriola Madorell in 1982. She has held lectures at Columbia and Gerona universities and at the Barcelona ETSA.

Monika Gora, born 1959, studied landscape architecture at Uppsala College of Agriculture, Sweden. She has worked as a freelance artist since 1988.

Bruno Flierl, born in 1927, graduated with doctorates in engineering and architecture after studies at the universities of the arts in Berlin and architecture in Weimar. He worked for the institute for theory and history of architecture of the academy of architecture of GDR, was the editor-in-chief of the journal Deutsche Architektur, and a lecturer in architecture and development at the Humboldt University in Berlin. Today he is a freelance architecture critic and architectural historian.

Feargus McGarvey is the President of the Irish Landscape Institute. He is an associate at Mitchell and Associates, and teaches landscape architecture at University College Dublin.

Willem Oomens is a freelance journalist. He also works for the architectural administration office of the Breda municipality. He has published on various urban planning and architectural projects.

Boris Podrecca, born in Belgrade in 1940, studied architecture at the Technical University and the Academy of Fine Arts in Vienna. He runs architecture offices in Vienna, Stuttgart and Venice, and has been a professor at the Technical University of Stuttgart since 1988.

Sophie Rousseau, born in 1957, studied architecture at the architectural university in Paris-Belleville. She works for public and private institutions as a researcher and international consultant in housing and urban planning. She has been teaching in the faculty of architecture at the Technical University of Eindhoven.

Robert Schäfer, born in 1954, studied landscape planning in Berlin and journalism in Stuttgart. He became editor-in-chief of Garten + Landschaft in 1985 and of Topos - European Landscape Magazine, which he founded, in 1992.

Photo Credits

J. Leone: 7
Gerard Dufresne : 8 right, 9
Jean-Pierre Charbonneau: 10 top, 11, 14 , 15 below
amc # 89+91: 10, 15
Andreas Muhs:18-29
Carmen Fiol: 30-35
Dennis Gilbert: 37-42
Peter Matthews: 44-47
Mitchell and Associates: 49
Barry Mason: 50
Peter Zöch: 51
Bernard Seymour: 53
Lars Gemzoe: 54, 59 right, 65
Stadsarkitektens Direktorat: 56 top, 57, 59 left, 60 top, 61, 62, 66; Stadsarkitektens Direktorat: 56 bottom, 58, 60 bottom, 63
Andreas Trier Morch: 55
Jens Lindhe: 68, 69
Ola Roe: 70-74
Jordi Bellmunt Chiva, Xavier Andreu Barrera: 75-79
Roberto Collovà: 80-87
Jeroen Musch: 88-94
Oskar Dariz: 95, 98
Alberto Lagomaggiore: 97, 100
Boris Podrecca: 99
Verkstaedi: 102-104
Karres en Brands: 105-107
Fotolino: 109
Monika Gora: 110-111
Thorbjörn Andersson: 112-120
Arthur Bagen: 121-126

Translations

Olaf Probst: 6
Lisa Diedrich: 30, 80, 88
Bettina del Chin: 75
Edith Walter: 37, 110
Ursula Poblotzki: 43, 48
Robert Schäfer: 70
Cornelia Groethuysen: 11
Beate Rupprecht: 105, 121
Edith Walter: 110
Almuth Seebohm: 5, 6, 18, 32, 54, 75, 88, 95, 121
Judith Harrison: 102, 105, 110

© 2002 Verlag Georg D. W. Callwey GmbH & Co. KG, Munich
in cooperation with Birkhäuser – Publishers for Architecture, P.O.Box 133, CH-4010 Basel, Switzerland

A CIP catalogue record for this book is available from the Library of Congress, Washington D.C., USA.

Deutsche Bibliothek Cataloging-in-Publication Data – CIP-Einheitsaufnahme

Plätze = Urban squares. - München : Callwey,
    ISBN 3-7667-1513-5

Printed on chlorine-free pulp. TCF

Printed in Germany

ISBN Callwey
3-7667-1513-5
ISBN Birkhäuser
3-7643-6670-2